# Beyond Mind

Essays, poems, opinions and humor on seeking
and finding answers to your deepest life-questions

# Beyond Death

Excerpts from the *TAT Forum*, an online
journal appearing at *www.tatfoundation.org*

Published by the TAT Foundation

*Beyond Mind, Beyond Death*

First Edition: 2009
Printed in the United States of America

Cover design: Paul Burns

Title page fonts: Goudy Handtooled BT; Times New Roman
Text font: Palatino Linotype
Special character fonts: Fleurons A, Griffin Regular, Asian Dings

Main entry under title: Beyond Mind, Beyond Death
Index included

1. Spirituality                2. Philosophy

Library of Congress Control Number: 2007909170

ISBN: 978-0-9799630-0-1

Visit our web site: www.tatfoundation.org

Note: The above symbol of the three stepped triangles represents the Jacob's Ladder diagram of the mind described by Richard Rose in *Psychology of the Observer*.

# INTRODUCTION

In November of 2000, the TAT Foundation began publishing a monthly online magazine of spiritual writings: the *TAT Forum*. This volume represents some of the best material from that monthly mix of essays, poetry and humor. In winnowing through seventy-seven issues and over eight hundred selections, our desire was to create a "desert island book"—a volume to cherish for a lifetime and revisit again and again for inspiration and guidance on the spiritual path.

We are seemingly born on an incoming tide and die with its outflow. What is the purpose of life? Of your life? Of death? What will bring lasting happiness or contentment? What will cure the ache in your heart? Is there a soul, a God, or anything other than this world of carnage and compassion? Around a corner that ever recedes we feel there is an answer to the numberless questions that haunt and drive our lives.

Many are the voices in this volume, from classic to contemporary, yet all point toward a greater reality than that of which we are typically aware—a Reality that can only be hinted at with words; that must and can be discovered by you rather than described by an author. This is the insistent and inspiring message of this work: that there is hope, there is an answer and discovery that satisfies for all time our life's longing. Let your journey begin, continue and end with these pages.

# Contents

# 1: THE STILL POINT OF THE TURNING WORLD

## The Still Point of the Turning World, by Bob Cergol

- What is the still point in your turning world?
- Have you found it? Have you been there?
- Do you know where it is? Can you go there anytime you want?
- Is it inside or outside?
- If it is inside, does that place you outside of it?

I want to talk about how you got to where you find yourself now—and this is really about your journey out of stillness and into increasing turmoil. Examining this will reveal much about where you are headed—and why. (Verbal communication about this sounds contradictory, so you have to see/feel your way past the grammatical paradox of these words that falsely imply a non-existent dichotomy.)

My fundamental premise is that "the stillness" or "the silence" is all that there is—truly. And you came out of it even as a cloud emerges from the invisible ether in the sky—and you will return to it in like fashion. Consequently it is at the very core of your nature to want to abide there—for that which is essentially still cannot remain in motion. In truth, that motion is merely an appearance of motion, and in reality you are not separate from that stillness or silence. Who—and what—you really are is at all times utterly still and absolutely silent.

Paradoxically, your seeking to satisfy this inner need expresses your striving to live in separation from your source and, simultaneously, expresses the source itself. Paradoxically, your seeking to satisfy this inner need is your greatest obstacle but, simultaneously, your way home. It is an obstacle because it is the project of the personal and validates the personal "you." But it is also your way home because the desire to seek is itself born from the inner being.

To most students of the esoteric sides of philosophy, religion and psychology, my words thus far may sound *all too familiar,* and that very fact brings us back to this question of how you got to where you find yourself now—to the "you" to which these words sound all too familiar.

Be aware, as we pursue this dialog, that there are always two dialogs going on, not just between me and you, here and now, but always within your own self. There is the dialog of the inner being with the outer being and the dialog of the outer being with itself. The dialog of the outer drowns out the inner, yet it cannot silence it. The outer dialog is like an echo—onto which your attention has become so fixated, trying desperately not to lose track of it before it ages into oblivion, that you have completely overlooked and forgotten the original, crystal clear, loud and immediately present source of that echo—the inner dialog. This inner dialog is between that which is the real, still and silent being that you and I are in common, and the outer being. These words are merely the echo of that inner dialog—and an echo of a rapport—wherein the voice speaking now, and the ears hearing now, are of one being—else no worthwhile communication is occurring. This inner dialog is not a dialog of words. There is no outer being—only a seeming of such, born of looking away. In the final analysis there is no dialog—only a seeming of such when the echo begins its journey home. The inner dialog is a beacon guiding the way. You have to listen, past the great rumbling generated by your quest to be—somebody and something. When the only thing you can hear is the still silence, then you have found what you are.

How do you find that truly still point? A Zen master once wrote, "There is only one way—you must abandon the egocentric position."

This egocentric position is so entrenched as our point of reference that it goes unnoticed despite all the books that you read about dropping egos. It goes unnoticed despite all the meditation disciplines you practice aimed at transcending thought and finding your real self. It goes unnoticed because somewhere along your journey it/you got the idea that defining yourself is achieved by addition (a dust cloud in a desert). All the great teachers tell us the path is through subtraction, but the egocentric position sees this as self-elimination. In truth this subtractive process is not self-elimination, it is the finding of the only thing that really is you.

## The Dawning of Identity—Experience Is Binding

A Zen master wrote that the ego projects an ego on which to work in order to preserve its own primacy; i.e., so long as you are working at fixing this ego, or altering it in some way, you are firmly protected from looking in the mirror. All eyes are focused, so to speak, on ego2 while ego1 remains unnoticed.

Try this experiment. Close your eyes. Notice how you feel right now—present in the body. Go ahead and feel the complete sense of the position of your body and any sense of comfort or lack of comfort. Now notice the feeling of being your self—the feeling of having an identity. Notice the sense of self-awareness that is present. This sense of self surrounds all perception and experience. You are you. You feel—"I am." This sense of self is behind all thought. I want you to focus your attention—not with worded thought—but with direct feeling of this sense of being you.

Now there's just one problem with this—and that is—that entire sense-of-self, that whole feeling of being you, that lovable "I-ness" is NOT going to survive death. You need to remind yourself of this because you have it in your head that it is the body that's not going to survive. Where—pray tell—are you going to live without your body?

Since you don't really believe this, if you are still focused keenly on that sense of "you" being here "now," ask yourself this question: From where does this sense of self arise? Where were you before your birth? Where will you be after your death?

Can you even put your finger on the essence of this sense-of-being without placing it in a personal context? Can you separate awareness from yourself without taking ownership of it?

This self-identity is not your real being. This sense of self is the egocentric position that takes ownership of everything—even of awareness. Do not mistake the two as the same. That personal identity is impermanent. Only the impersonal awareness that powers it is permanent. The self you feel yourself to be right now is impermanent. It is entirely dependent upon an impersonal awareness. Do not invert reality. That identity felt as the sense-of-self does not possess awareness. Awareness is entirely independent of it. When you hold to the notion that you possess awareness, you cannot imagine awareness absent your personal identity.

When that mortal self realizes and accepts this distinction, something profoundly magical occurs: what remains is awareness alone, and a sense of abiding in utter silent stillness—there is the sense that the entire world is but a reflection of an underlying absolute, silent, stillness. This awareness is referred to by Franklin Merrell-Wolff as "consciousness without an object," i.e., with no dependence upon physical perceptions and thoughts, indeed without that sense of personal identity which is itself a thought.

Richard Rose writes: "The task of the seeker of eternity is to die while living." The mortal seeker, in truly accepting his mortality, realizes that there is nothing to die and that only that which is eternal ever existed in the first place. So long as the seeker must live, then he must live in mortal separation from eternity.

The sense of self-as-identity is the focus in awareness on experience brought about by the body experience—and it overlays the focus on the ever present, silent stillness in which this sense of self occurs. The sense of self-identity, occurring in awareness, is entirely dependent upon experience. Your entire sense of self is merely an experience! The body/mind is an experience machine. You think to yourself, "Ah, but that experience must be happening to somebody—and that somebody is ME!" Once again the egocentric point of reference has got it backwards. It is the body/mind experiences that give rise to the sense of self-identity. The body will die and be dissipated. The mind is at all times one with the body and will likewise be dissipated. When that happens what will remain of "he-who-experiences"? Answer: Nothing of you will remain.

The story of a man's life in a very real sense is the story of this character reconciling itself to this immutable fact—which it knows in its heart of hearts to be true. Each individual's life's story is the story of coping with and comforting oneself—while dying a slow death. We are—all of us—dying a slow death.

## The Building of Identity—Striving to Define Oneself

You are born into this world as an individual body, and just as that body does not contain air so much as it is immersed in an ocean of air, so too is it immersed in the all-pervasive Silent Stillness—the Living Awareness.

It is this background of Awareness in which the process of experience occurs and gives rise to separate individual consciousness. The physical body is a sense perception machine. The first perceptual experience simultaneously gives rise to the subject "having" the experience. Experience builds on experience and identity builds on identity.

You experience individuality and until proven otherwise know only that you exist as an individual. To exist as an individual—and consequently, to feel the compulsion from a source unknown—to be that individual—while at the same time not knowing just what exactly that individuality is, or is supposed to be—means that you have no choice but to define yourself to yourself. (Identity spins identity.) That is your nature, period. That is the direction of all your thoughts and actions. This imperatve is itself an expression of, or an echo of, that Being, from which all arises, when manifested as individualized forms—a dust funnel in a desert.

When you think you are looking inward, you are in fact looking outward. You can never really see yourself. The instant that such seeing occurs will be the same instant that the self you take yourself to be will cease to exist. The direction of your looking is to define, build, magnify and preserve this self—generated by experience.

This is a hopeless endeavor since by definition that self doesn't know what it is and therefore what to preserve. The method of preservation is to possess all in its field of vision and by association with the "real" out there infer its own reality. All the poignant pathos in your life is the story of this process.

## Identity Spins Identity

Here's your predicament:

Childhood launched you on a journey of creating your individuality. You were the center of the universe, and the universe existed to satisfy you. The world had to conform to you. You create the world in your own image and likeness.

Adolescence launched you on a journey to find your relationship to the world—further defining your individuality. By now the world had also become a threat to that individuality, and fear became entrenched. You now also had to conform to the world.

In young adulthood you seek to find your role in that world, and your possibilities seem endless. Now cautious that the world can also be your enemy, you still see the purpose of the world as serving your needs. The only problem is how—what pathway are you supposed to take. It gradually becomes more and more apparent that you have little control over the outcome. It's starting to look like the world is stronger than you are. You steel—or resign—yourself and determine to forge ahead to live your life, to continue the process of building your individuality—albeit with some level of doubt.

But before you can commit, a terrible indecision begins to arise like a worm eating away from the inside. There is the fear of taking the wrong path. There is the hesitation in lack of conviction that any given direction is the way you are supposed to go. Why? What is this fear?

So long as your possibilities were endless and the purpose of the world was to serve you, you were safe. But now the world is recognized as much, much bigger than yourself and you must somehow find your place in it.

You cannot dispel the doubt that the quest to build your individuality ultimately cannot succeed because it won't make your individuality bigger and longer lasting than the world. In fact the world itself might swallow you up. You are threatened from within and from without.

Your indecision and uncertainty stem from the recognition somewhere deep inside of your own mortality. Your whole life you have managed to look away from the fact of your own mortality. You fear that your time is limited and that you will not be able to go back. But it is also the awareness that you're not even sure of what it is you are trying to build and protect.

A conscious life-long commitment, such as raising a family, is difficult to make because once made it fixes the end-point. Death becomes real enough that it is no longer as completely out of your consciousness.

So the outer dialog says, "Choose wisely. You have one shot at crossing the chasm."

But the inner dialog says, "All things betray thee, who betrayest Me."

## The Denial of Death

It's a fact, you can lie to everyone around you, but you cannot lie to yourself. The only thing you can do is look away from whatever you don't want to face.

Therefore the only thing to do is to face everything squarely—and it is the looking away from the ever-present fact of death that is the fundamental problem.

Our life's story is really about our journey of learning how to reconcile ourselves with, and accept, our own death.

## The Path

Use the "Who am I?"

Focus the attention on sensation and feeling, not on thoughts. Do not focus the attention on emotions per se, but on the sensation of having the feeling—both the sensation of having the feeling and the source of the feeling.

Thoughts generated by this attempt are the reaction to this "direct looking," and the "looking away" is experienced as a rush of ensuing thoughts.

## How Did You Get to Where You Find Yourself Right Now?

This is an exercise in trying to see and feel, not think.

What is the *earliest* memory that occurs to you now of "you as a child"?
What is the circumstance?
What is the feeling?
Can you see what your thoughts were then?

What memory occurs to you now of "you as an adolescent"?
What is the circumstance?
What is the feeling?
Can you see what your thoughts were then?

What memory occurs to you now of "you as a young adult"?
What is the circumstance?
What is the feeling?
Can you see what your thoughts were then?

What memory is most prominent of "you last year"?
What is the circumstance?
What is the feeling?
Can you see what your thoughts were then?

*Bob gave this as a workshop presentation at the Self Knowledge Symposium's Avila Retreat in November 2001.*

## Who Says Words with My Mouth?
### by Jelaluddin Rumi (translated by Coleman Barks)

All day I think about it, then at night I say it.
Where did I come from, and what am I supposed to be doing?
I have no idea.
My soul is from elsewhere, I'm sure of that,
and I intend to end up there.

This drunkenness began in some other tavern.
When I get back around to that place,
I'll be completely sober. Meanwhile,
I'm like a bird from another continent, sitting in this aviary.
The day is coming when I fly off,
but who is it now in my ear who hears my voice?
Who says words with my mouth?

Who looks out with my eyes? What is the soul?
I cannot stop asking.
If I could taste one sip of an answer,
I could break out of this prison for drunks.
I didn't come here of my own accord,
  and I can't leave that way.
Whoever brought me here will have to take me home.

This poetry. I never know what I'm going to say.
I don't plan it.
When I'm outside the saying of it,
I get very quiet and rarely speak at all.

## *The Black Wall, by Shawn Nevins*

Death is inside each of us. I don't mean that we will all die one day. I mean that if we peer inside, down the mazy layers of noise that pass for a mind, we discover a black wall of the unknown. Behind this, inside us, is death.

Light masquerades as darkness inside you—true Life as death. I don't know why. I don't know why it is easier to look away, toward the mischief of the world, than inside. Yet the resolution of our driving questions is inside. By turning away from that which you see in the field of the mind (since anything you see cannot be you), you will surely travel to these dark gates.

That is the essence of the approach. It starts with the proposition that anything observable is not us. What you see through a microscope is not the microscope, and what you see via the mind is not the mind. "The view is not the viewer," Richard Rose said, though for years I couldn't grasp what he meant. However, I did understand that anything observable is not permanent, and that is what I wanted to know: what about me would not change and fade away—was there anything Real?

"Not this, not that," as the Upanishads said over 2,500 years ago. I am not that cup of water on the table. I am not the hand typing this sentence. I am not these words appearing in my mind. I am not awareness. This may take years to grasp. You can't just conclude. You have to experience. You have to look inside your mind and decide for yourself.

Again and again you go a-searching, rejecting every thought as not you, every sound or vision, and your sense of self even, because you see them all in your mind's eye. Yet, some thing turns away from all these objects—an awareness that is impossibly aware of itself and senses something else behind it. It tries to turn upon itself only to find itself. It—you—have come to the black wall.

The image of the black wall is indicative of what I sensed. It was an unknown around which my awareness pirouetted with itself—a desperate dance at the dead end street of the mind. You may explain the feeling with a different image—perhaps simply as fear, or wonder, or perplexity, or intense tension as if trying to grasp infinity or zero.

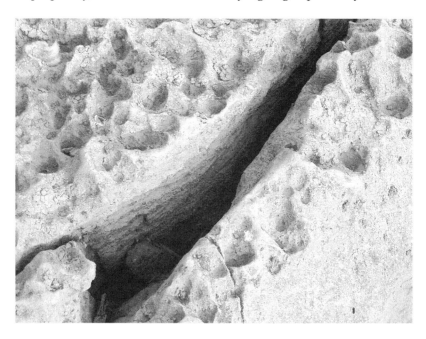

The method of rejecting what we see as not us takes us directly to the fundamental uncertainty of our self-knowledge. That fundamental uncertainty hides behind the fear of extinction. Your life of honesty and determination will carry you through this wall, through death, to Life.

Following are two quotes that strike at the heart of going within. They challenged and inspired me to keep looking:

Am I this body of thoughts in my mind? No. One gets a little closer to his thoughts than to anything else, and it's a little harder to untangle this. But if he watches and studies closely enough, the thoughts come to me. I accept or reject them. That which accepts or rejects them is different from the thought. And then I finally reach this point where I find that I must be this something, in some sense, different from other people. I'm not the mind, I'm not the feelings, I'm not the body—that I see. But I surely *am*, I surely am an individual, apart from others.

Now what you've gotten a hold of is a very difficult fellow—it's your ego. He can sneak around and confuse you like the dickens. You can spend years trying to get behind him. And what you do, you can get into an infinite regression. You look at your ego. All right, here am I and all of a sudden it dawns upon you that *that* which is looking at the ego is really the I. So you stick that one out in front. You look at it again, but then you realize it couldn't be, because here is a something that is observable. At last it finally dawns that I AM THAT which is *never* an object before Consciousness. And mayhap, at that moment, in your analysis—the Heavens will open. ~ Franklin Merrell-Wolff, *The Induction*

From this point, as we look to the right, we notice that we can also look at awareness, and we can be aware of consciousness, and of looking at ourself looking indefinitely. We do not take a step forward, but are taken forward from here, by that which seems to be an accident—an accident which does not come unless we have struggled relentlessly to find that which was unknown to us, by a method which could not be charted because the end or goal was unknown. We must have first become a vector. We must first have spent a good period of time studying our own awareness and consciousness with our own consciousness until we accidentally or by some unknown purpose—enter the source of our awareness. ~ Richard Rose, *Psychology of the Observer*

## *Tears for Fears, by Bob Fergeson*

We climb inside our pride to hide,
digging holes to crawl inside.
To run from Fear inside a tear,
we run inside our Pride to hide.

Why does life seem so hard to try?
Turn left, back right,
I can't decide.
Fear blocks my skill, what's left, pride kills,
I run inside vast pride to hide.
At the end of every year
I shed a tear for every fear
that drives poor souls the whole world wide
to crawl inside their pride to hide.

The warning whispered in Caesar's ear
should not have been for a time of year
but to give him heed to that inside,
Oh, Caesar! Keep watch on the Ides of Pride.

Where are my father, mother, siblings three?
They all have sailed far out to sea,
driven by fear and self-tyranny,
they sailed back into pride, you see.
To build stone towers on islands each,
to fly the flag of pride above the breach.
This, they hope, keeps fear back 'cross the moat
but ties their souls with tight black ropes.
And safe within their castle keep,
safe from fear, safe in sleep,
kept prisoner by Fear's mighty tide,
they lie inside their pride and hide.

Cry humble tears where the paradox lies,
not boast of things that live, then die.
Come forth to stand in the light of day,
your gaze looks back on the world of clay,
no fear, no moan, no cry of dismay.

Climb out the trench where we all lie,
stand firm in Truth, don't fear the lies.
Shake off the dark, dank cloud of pride.

Don't fight too hard, don't try to hide, just
let it be, this curse of Pride.
To Humble be's a trick you see,
it leads you round to Pride's vast sea.

# 2: Clouds of Consciousness

### *Ghost in a Box, by Bob Fergeson*

In the realm of spiritual seekers, many and varied are the conceptions of what the Final Realization will be. Most of these are meaningless discussions of symptoms rather than any serious attempt at understanding the final state, much less becoming It. The projected outcomes of these students are as varied as the different schools and teachers in which they place their trust. Given this Gordian Knot of thinking and feeling, fueled by ego, and projected by unexamined minds, what can one do, and expect? How can a serious seeker find assurance that they are on the right course, and how can one be sure that they themselves, or someone they know and trust, has had the Final Realization, a Total Answer?

First off, the final judge must be the person themselves. In order to pass beyond the duality of the finite mind, we must be aware of the trap of putting yet one more level above us. This is a never-ending game of the mind. There will always be someone out there who claims to have a higher, more complete, more total realization than what we, or our teacher, may have found. Only in our Selves can we rest. The trap of endlessly judging levels of attainment may be a way to keep our own spiritual ego afloat, but is a dangerous distraction if taken as the quest itself. We must press on within, and leave the fate of others to themselves.

The above said, there still remains the problem of the mind's ability to fool itself with its own projections. Driven by ambition, mental laziness, and fear of the Unknown, we may unconsciously decide to claim realization by virtue of these desires and fears, and take an easy out. How can we check and compare our own level of spiritual attainment and not be misled, by our mind or the minds of others? Let us take a look at the stages of spiritual becoming, and hope that the words herein will serve as a guide to keep our vector moving and on track.

There are three states or levels of being that we find in this search, before reaching what might be called the final or absolute state.

The first may be called the level of experience. The second, the level of union. The third, the level of becoming.

The first level, that of experience, may be likened to someone in his room watching a television, and being identified with the characters in the dramas as they unfold on the screen. Losing contact with himself, he has become hypnotized into believing he is a character in the TV. The freedom he began with, that he *was* (and still Is), the innocent observer, has been lost, traded for the mind-motion of thought and feeling projected into the plastic box in front of him. He places his highest value on the screen-character with the most motion and energy, in relation to his upbringing and education by other screen characters. The more the characters move and are dominant (whether positive or negative does not matter), the more energy is expended and the bigger the reaction that is drawn from the person. His innocence and detachment have been replaced with the sense of motion and thought, and the thrill of losing energy. Now that he is inseparable from his role in the drama, he places a high meaning on the feeling of belonging, which he now values as part of his very definition. He has fallen deep into sleep and is dreaming the life he thinks he lives, a mere ghost in a box of motion, emotion and thought. He will evaluate a mystical experience in much the same way. If the experience has much motion, much release of energy, and if the character involved succeeds in his tasks, whether positive or negative, he will place a higher value on him and claim his identity for his own.

This level is very basic and body-oriented, having to do with visions of power and ego and control over the environment. Any mystical experience or contact with spiritual systems or teachers a person on this level has will be interpreted from this level. It constitutes no real change, or becoming, in what might be called the basic animal man, who, perhaps frustrated in his ambitions in normal life and society, has chosen a path of lesser resistance through fantasy for the fulfillment of his animal urge to power and dominance. He is the level of the mind and its motion, with which he is wholly identified. Fear and desire drive his every move, and he is firmly engrossed in his dreams.

The second level is only found through the disastrous failure of the first, combined with a serious inner commitment the seeker must have previously made to finding the truth about himself at any cost.

Given this commitment, he will sooner or later be rudely shaken awake from his dreams of fantasy and forced to face the facts about himself. For a true change to occur, a true failure of the first level's ego must be brought about. His sense of personal identity, which is rooted in the fictional characters in the box, one after another, must be cut away. The resulting trauma will be in proportion to the size of the ego that was created. The symptoms of this collapse, meaning emotional and mental trauma, are individual and should not be taken as the change itself.

The possibility of the inner witness coming closer to the surface is the only important matter. The man then becomes identified with not just the individual character(s) on the screen of the TV as it continues to hold him entranced but now becomes identified with everything that enters the universe-box from the projecting Light. His sense of self expands to include all the characters in the drama as he gains a sense of unity with all the many dots in their coordinated dance across the screen. He may feel exalted and full of love for this picture show and imagine this union to be the end-all of possibility. His very sense of exaltation, of still clinging to a higher and lower, with his remaining sense of being a 'being," give him away. The experience, though of a greater level than that of the first man, is still relative. He still believes himself to be a thing apart, in contact with another, though higher, Thing apart. The very idea of existence, of himself and anything else, is still intact, and unquestioned. His new profound experience is just that, and it fades into a memory, though the conviction may remain. He soon finds himself back in the position of the first man, in motion and identified, subject to the environment for his feeling and concept of himself in the moment. Only in his memory and understanding is there a change. His perspective is still that of a man, a human entity, alive and living in a now conscious Cosmos, with which he is united.

For the man of union to Become, he must again suffer a complete disaster and have an impossible bit of good luck, to boot. Through somehow seeing the still remaining dual nature of his mind, he may find the hint within that there is something of the intuition, which led him this far, still in contact with him. He may see from time to time that he senses he is somehow behind himself, apart and unconcerned with the "thing" that he previously called "I." He may even experience moments of "headlessness," in which he looses his usual sense of "self" and instead sees the world without the noisy filter of his mind. He may even have the intuition that the secret to Becoming lies in this detachment and not in the blissful union he values so much. This detachment has yet to become a steady factor in the present moment, but he begins to sense that the unaffected yet somehow aware screen, the very *capacity* for existence, and not the mind-made images that run across it in an ever-changing flux, is his true nature; that the Light and the screen it illuminates are but two different aspects of the same thing: Himself. Intuition now plays the bigger part, with reason and logic now only functions of the practical aspect of his environment.

Many little hints may come to him now, and if he is lucky enough to place a value on them, and follow them, he will continue to move. Most of these hints are along the lines of what has been called "headlessness" or the "listening attention." He may find he is observing without labeling or judging. That he is now free, for a moment, to gaze upon the world without knowing what he sees. These moments may be accompanied by a strange feeling of peace or silence, which he may come to know as the quiescence of his mind. Here, the former work on fear and desire come to fruit, as one cannot look into the Unknown if any vestige of fear or worldly ambition are still dominant. The sight of the world without the mind's interpretation can be frightening for those still attached to its false security. By continuing to look within, he may sense that the Light he feels is not only healing him but has a direction, a Source. If he travels back far enough to merge with this Source, he may find It to be the opposite of the "world" and hence come to the possibility of triangulating the difference between Samsara and Nirvana, and so coming to Himself as that which contains, and simultaneously is, All.

This return to our original nature extracts a high price, but only to the ghost in the plastic box. The ego, which has evolved from identification with the character on the screen to that of the ego of the spirit united with its source, now has died. For the original awareness, this is release, yet it finds itself to be unchanged and knows it has never been any different. To friends and family, the symptoms of this final ego-death may, or may not, be visibly dramatic. The trauma of release is indicative of the size of the ego that dies rather than of the nature of the underlying Reality. Any value we place on the size or spectacle of the resulting trauma of others may be due to our own need for distraction and longing for continued sleep in our pride as sincere seekers. Facing our own coming headlessness is much more difficult than ruminating about the possible symptoms of the decapitation of others. Much of what may have happened in another's becoming may not have been made available for our personal viewing and consequent judgment.

The worded description of this final state is something that has caused much consternation in seekers and teachers alike through the centuries. Perhaps the best that can be said about it is what it is not. It is not an intellectual conclusion reached through deduction, no matter how astute. It is not a feeling-state, no matter how sublime. It is something we receive, though we give it to ourselves. We become It rather than "get it" and then know we have never not been It.

In most schools, words such as *awareness, witness, absolute* and *void* are used to describe the causeless state, which we seek to become: an aware witness, void of any other qualities; an unbiased, empty Observer, having no cause, but being the cause of Itself, alone; a conditionless yet aware state that is itself unconditioned and not witnessable by other than itself, there being nothing other than Itself. Any description one hears which adds a word or words after "I am" is not a description of the Self but, at most, a description of a symptom or view. Be very wary of those who claim unending Bliss and Peace, for any relative state calls forth its opposite and is subject to change. You, and only you, will come to know what your final state is, and then, later, you will struggle to find words to describe it.

## *The Key, by Jim Burns*

- What is the most important thing for me to think about at this moment?
- Give yourself the ability to *be* the answer.
- "Knock, and it shall be opened." Give it enough time.
- Draw yourself up to zero. It's a problem of the animal—the body and mind are afraid to be still.
- The key was finding that I should not try to direct my awareness. I had to let the light within direct me to the light within.

*Conversation excerpts from the July 2003 TAT meeting.*

## *Clouds of Consciousness, by Gary Harmon*

The emergence of a cloud materializing out of the breath of nowhere is similar to the way we have appeared, and the way we will dissipate, also. Clouds appear and disappear, they are born and they die. It can be said that they transform continually but their essence remains the same. Without any planning or particular reason, clouds just materialize.

As I watch the different types of clouds floating across the sky, there is a sense of kinship. We have much in common with the "life" of a cloud. Immortality is a prime feature of the evident transitory existence. They change from a vapor to a visible form, changing again from detectable form back to a diffusion of vapors. There is an eternal implication to the entire procedure. Our life cycle is a very similar process with no memory of the place that we have appeared from; we just become conscious of our existence. How magnificent and astounding this actually is.

Here is a contribution by Pei-chien (1185-1246), a Cloud of Consciousness that dissipated long ago. His words are just as alive as when they were first written:

> Let your actions be like clouds going by; the clouds
> going by are mindless. Let your stillness be as the
> valley spirit; the valley spirit is undying. When
> action accompanies stillness and stillness combines
> with action, then the duality of action and stillness
> no longer arises.

It can be understood that consciousness is very sky-like. There is nothing to observe at all, just the unoccupied, measureless space. Out of nowhere a cloud appears in the atmosphere, in quite the same manner that we are created out of emptiness. The cloud always remains part of the sky, just as we forever remain a vector of empty space.

## *Poems by Shawn Nevins*

A river of words moves among us
bringing this mind to life.
My soul parts these waters,
choosing words that love
to settle into the space beyond words,
that ask you to listen
to this...
ending and beginning.

A snake crawls curling his way
through dry sands.

What does he know of truth?
What thoughts follow his tongue?
Who sees with those unblinking eyes?

He runs his pale belly over a knife's edge,
spilling dreams over the void.
His eyes begin to shine.

A tired warrior may find a friend
amidst a field of weeds,
honest in the face of winter,
and that is enough.

As I turn within
everything around me
becomes the image of God.

The particular loses its meaning
and gains Significance.
Every motion attests to silence,
as a single leaf's fall
slices open the picture —
without and within dissolves.

A tree is more honest
when stripped of its leaves
and stark against the sky.
Otherwise it hides among its neighbors
in a confusion of leaves.
Leafless, we see its progress
and where it intends to go.

Be without adornment
and the distraction of personal seasons.

All words arise in mid feeling
and circle round *This Place*
like smoke.

Be who you are,
alone with me,
where words such as you and I matter not.
The lightest touch of the mind
splits nothingness in two.
Such is the trouble with the power of God
in the hands of children.
Listen.
What is true sounds like this....

## *Critical Path to Nirvana, Art Ticknor*

The path to Nirvana is as simple as 1-2-3.

The starting point is dissatisfaction, which can take on many shapes and hues. It may be tied to a fear of what death will bring, for example, or a deep disturbance at the perceived lack of meaning or purpose in your life, or an intolerable doubt that you are what you think you are.

Step #1 is intuiting, or hearing and believing, that all answers lie within. If you're fortunate, this intuition or belief will also include the understanding that you don't find the answer but become it.

Step #2 is turning the focus of your attention around until you find yourself looking at what you're looking out from.

Step #3 is admitting or accepting the implications of what is seen in step #2.

The critical path diagram is theoretically as simple as:

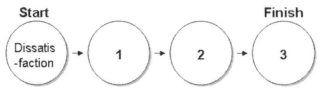

But this process or progression is not something that can be understood by the mind or managed by the individual. Even getting from dissatisfaction to step #1 is not something that we can *do* or force to occur. The vast majority of humanity will not be so fortunate as to reach step #1.

Moving on from point #1 to point #2 is the part of the path or "the way" that gets the most attention in the literature of spiritual work. The consensus view is that this is an arduous journey with many hazards, and the truth is that few people who start the journey complete it. Franklin Merrell-Wolff was convinced that for each individual there is a shortest path—and that finding that shortest path depends on applying intuition to customize the tools or techniques needed to continue the journey to fit one's own peculiarities. Richard Rose referred to his similar conviction as "creating the ways and means committee."

Douglas Harding had a profound experience of seeing what he was looking out from at age 33, after which he devoted his life to developing and demonstrating experiments that would give people their first conscious glimpse of this direct seeing. Some people "get it" upon first exposure to one or more of the experiments, which might be described as thought-experiments that take you beyond thought. So it's possible that moving from step #1 to step #2 could occur rapidly.

Something has to break the hypnotic spell that keeps our focus outward, whether that "outside" is the physical dimension or the mental dimension. If something like Harding's experiments—and I don't know of anything else like them—don't do it for you, either by lack of exposure to them or lack of impact, then you're faced with a potentially long haul with no guarantees. Success once again depends on factors beyond our control. First, you must have or find *faith* that you can find a total answer, or faith that nothing else is more worthwhile than devoting your life to trying. Second, you must have or find the determination to stick with what will seem, at some point, like an absurd or hopeless task, like Don Quixote's jousting with windmills.

Somehow the focus of attention has to be turned around so that you "retraverse the ray of creation" in Rose's poetic phrasing. This may involve bringing the mind under control, which can't be done directly. Rose's recommendation was to learn to turn the attention away from irrelevant thoughts in order to do *productive thinking* about the problem—the problem being lack of adequate self-definition or knowing what we really are. By doing so, this may bring a temporary halt to thinking, opening the possibility to an experience of direct seeing such as Harding's vision at age 33. Rose was a proponent of stopping thought, as was Ch'an master Huang Po. Merrell-Wolff, on the other hand, found it didn't work for him. He concluded that it was a common recommendation because most people arrived mainly from the feeling side, whereas his own path was mainly from the thought or intellectual side.

"What prevents this observing of the observer or looking at what we're looking out from? How can I do it?" It's what we really are at center, so in a sense there's nothing preventing it. It's accessible to anyone when they stop turning away from it. But it's not something we can *will* or *do*. You might ask yourself whenever the how-to question comes up—and the more often it comes up, the better—"What is more compelling to me at this moment? What business do I feel I have to attend to first? What excuses do I provide myself? What side trips have I been taking?"

When you reach step #2 and find yourself looking at what you're looking out from—observing the observer—you may not "enter nirvana" immediately. Nirvana or the kingdom of heaven is not a paradisiacal place you gain entry to. The term literally means a blowing out, or extinction. It may take repeated seeing of what you really are at center before you admit or accept the implications. "Wait a minute," you may find yourself thinking, "I see that what I am is self-aware and contains all existence … but I'm the observer that sees this." To reach step #3 and cross the finish line from great dissatisfaction to Full Satisfaction, something has to get blown out. And this thing that gets extinguished is the final holdout: the spiritual ego, the conviction that I, as observer, am a thing apart.

*Note: While it reportedly took less than an hour for Ramana Maharshi, at age 17, to go from point #1 to the finish line (in the preface to* The Collected Works of Ramana Maharshi *edited by Arthur Osborne), it took Merrell-Wolff 24 years, to age 48 or 49. Douglas Harding's journey lasted 44 years, until age 77, if I understood him correctly. Richard Rose accomplished it in about 9 years, at the age of 30. Don't make the mistake of setting up a timetable for this project.*

*"Every night, half of the people in the first row are crying when the star is singing* To Dream the Impossible Dream. *It's sad to see successful, middle-aged men with tears streaming down their faces, regretting that they didn't pursue their 'impossible' dreams." ~ An oboe player in the orchestra of* The Man from La Mancha *(the stage play based on Don Quixote's life).*

### Last Supper, by Art Ticknor

Surrounded by friends one last time,
No more arrivals or departures.
Movement ceases,
Silence prevails.
A solitary tear
Halts on its downward journey.
Sorrow blends into joy.
Knowing melts into unknowing.
Color recedes with the observer.
Anxiety fades into Peace.

# 3: Insight

## *Using Time Wisely, by Shawn Nevins*

People often don't realize the ways they could maximize their efforts. Small habits of inefficiency bog down the spiritual search. There are ways to let your search seep into every aspect of your life. A line from the great photographer Ansel Adams' autobiography comes to mind: "Whether I walk at Point Lobos, fly in an airplane, move in a new environment, or *relax* [my emphasis] in my home, I am always seeking to relate one shape or value to another, seeing an image in my mind's eye. It is a glorious and rewarding exploration." It takes time, but eventually you find that even while relaxing you can work on some aspect of your quest.

For example, I used to read a little from a spiritually themed book before I went to sleep. I believed that one's last thoughts before sleep would influence their dreams. Why not fill those six or eight hours of sleep with dreams of significance rather than of chasing women or other frantic running? Some find that they can go to sleep with a problem on their mind and a solution appears during the night.

In the morning, forgo the news at breakfast and read a book, listen to inspiring music, or practice Vipassana's mindful eating (see Goldstein's *The Experience of Insight*). Your mind will be more alert and attentive. It will provide meaningful thoughts to fill those moments during the day that you normally mull over worries or petty conflicts.

While commuting, listen to lectures on tape or ride in silence rather than wasting time with talks shows, news, or pop music. Douglas Harding has a meditation for driving that gives insight into one's true nature.

Curtail daydreaming with a mantra or prayer. I was so plagued by senseless daydreams that I took to heart Richard Rose's advice to think of nothing rather than tolerate rambling thoughts. I would count from one to ten, over and over, until the daydreams receded.

Skip the lunchtime gossiping and find a quiet place to break the work or school state of mind. You fall into habitual patterns of thought at work and school that you only see if you step outside and get a breath of fresh air. You remind your self what is truly important.

When in the mood to talk, find a spiritual friend. Discuss your latest endeavors, rather than talk sports or what's happening at work. Or take a different approach and ask your self why you feel the need to talk. Do you really have something you want to say, or are you burning off nervous energy that could be saved and channeled to your ultimate goal?

Let your exercise double as time for self-observation (notice when your body wants to stop exercising, how if you keep pushing the body goes along with your desire, and how that same pattern of action and resistance applies in other areas of your life), reviewing your reactions throughout the day, or as a moving meditation. Simply watching the muscles move is amazing. Try to determine when you consciously move the muscles. Where did the thought to raise your arm originate? Who decided when your arm would stop moving? Watch closely.

If you are exhausted or feeling ill and choose to watch TV or a movie, pick something thought provoking rather than completely escapist. I was haunted by Rose's line, "If you need entertainment, you are asleep."

There are interesting and inventive experiments to conduct while doing mundane chores. Use your meals to test the effects of different foods upon your thinking or your energy level. Observe people while grocery shopping. Test your intuition about what people will do or say. At any time, practice awareness of your thoughts and look for their cause and origin. Make notes of patterns of thoughts—thoughts you have around certain people, places, or situations. Break up your routines by driving or walking a different route. Smile when you are sad, or frown when happy. Notice and remember the results of your experiments. Keep a notepad handy to record your observations and inspirations.

The cumulative motion of these moments of seeking build your self into a vector—they forge a direction for your life. Like learning to type, one day you realize you no longer need typing exercises. You simply type. What requires effort at one point eventually becomes relatively effortless. Especially since, as your wisdom increases, your sense of doing anything decreases. To paraphrase Richard Rose: you simply seek the truth because you are a seeker of truth; not because you want any particular result. You become a humble, ego-less vector.

Some will fear this approach as too Spartan and extol the virtues of simply being and relaxing. Don't worry. You won't ever have a problem wasting time. The world is filled with passionless people passing the time, their lives, away. That is why this essay won't affect many people. Some understand the importance of self knowledge, a few intuit the immense depth of their self ignorance, and only a lucky few follow with determination their inner passion for an answer. "It is a glorious and rewarding exploration," for those lucky few.

## There Is No Death, by Bob Cergol

There is no death—because there is nothing to die. But we don't accept this because we want this identity to live—to be real. Accepting that there is nothing to die is acknowledging that the "we" we take as us is not—and the reality of that, we perceive as death!

## Silence, by Bob Fergeson

Silence has long been said to be a necessary component to any spiritual path, if not the goal itself. Much has been written of the Quiet, from its physical aspects, to using it as a symbol of the Void. Let us take a look at this thing called silence, and see if we may come to a better understanding of it, perhaps even to see it as it is, in ourself.

Silence can be said to have four aspects, in that it provides the background for the manifestation of four functions of mind. The first is the silence of the physical world, the realm of the body and senses. The next two are the silence of our emotions, within the heart, and the silence of the mind, behind the realm of thought. And finally, that of the spirit, the silence of awareness. As we come to know these aspects, we separate from the mind-function or foreground, and begin to travel within. Each one will be more difficult to accept than the last. We may see we actually fear silence, as it threatens us in our very sense of being, or identification. But as each fear is overcome and a new level reached, we may come to know that the Peace that passeth all understanding is found not in noise, form, emotion, or even in disciplined thought, but in silence.

The most common aspect of silence is its physical one, being the absence of physical sound. We can easily see the value of this in our seeking. Having a quiet place to meditate and think is a necessity for us when starting out on the path. We can concentrate, remember our goals, and look inside without outer distraction as we begin the arduous task of coming to know ourselves. This silence can be increasingly hard to come by in this day and age, being bombarded with noise in the form of entertainment and distraction as well as from the environment. We have become a society which places value on constant noise, making us afraid of the quiet, perhaps without even knowing why. Though this lack of environmental silence is prevalent, it is relatively easily dealt with compared with the mental and emotional aspects. To find a quiet place may take time and energy, but it does not require much in the way of facing ourselves, within. While the silence of the outer world may be threatening to some, it holds no place compared to the threat of the silence within.

All miseries derive from not being able
to sit quietly in a room alone. - *Pascal*

Emotional silence is found by bringing our feelings into consciousness. The unconscious emotional turmoil many of us experience leaves us no peace inside, and no ability to use our feelings as a true guide. Being unquestioned, they take on a life of their own, to which we say "I," and never gain any resolution of them in the moment. These feelings may drive us relentlessly in circles, never allowing us peace, clarity, or the ability to hold to a steady purpose. To find the goal or aim of our very life, the thing we came here for, is impossible without some level of silence within our heart. We may be desperately searching for something we have never defined, driven by anxieties of which we are mostly unconscious, and which serve no real need other than to tap our energy. Working our way back to a silent heart is a wondrous thing, indeed. There we may find a goal we can live and die with.

A quiet mind cureth all. - *Robert Burton*

Many are the systems and methods designed to quiet the mind, to reach an inner silence. Why is this? We are told that a quiet mind is paramount in achieving liberation, but just how is this defined? Is it an absence of thought, or the absence of identification with thought?

We may find that after training ourselves to "not think," that we have merely become good at holding the thought of "not thinking." This forced "silence" is not going to take us to the truth of ourselves. If we can find instead the true background silence behind the mind, then the thoughts may flow on without our being identified with them, enabling us to get a good look at them as they pass by. Thus we have become a silent observer of thought and mind, and taken a step farther within.

By witnessing our thoughts, rather than trying to control them, we begin to notice the endless internal dialogue running in our heads. Tricked into taking sides in this dialogue, we fight ourselves, pitting one thought-pattern against another, trapped in confusion. We may see that the next step into silence is found by simply listening, while paying careful attention. This may be terrifying to some, for it can threaten us at the level of our individuality, the ego itself, for now the voices of intuition and conscience may arise unhindered.

> The first step should be into silence. Begin with the
> silent witnessing of your thoughts. - *Vicki Woodyard*

We can see that by listening within, in the background of our mind, new information is available to us that was being drowned out by the internal dialogue, our "knowing," and the constant emotional dissonance. By allowing our innate intelligence, reason, and intuition to solve the problems of the mind as they surface, rather than fostering interference through unquestioned desires and fears running counter to our aim, we no longer force the mind to fight itself, leaving it relatively quiet and efficient. And perhaps surprisingly, we find we are no longer identified with it, and find again another silence, a silence of the spirit which contains the mind, rather than being contained by it.

> What is spiritual silence? It is not just the
> absence of talk. Silence has substance. It is
> the presence of something. - *Kathryn Damiano*

Here, beyond the reach of mind and emotions, we see we have become a silence, one that is aware. This is what Douglas Harding would call *aware capacity*. We have become the space in which all may happen. Just like the silence of the physical universe is the background and foundation of all noise, as the silence behind the notes allows the music to come into being, we have become that which gives existence to form and thought. As this aware silence, we may turn our attention around, and as we look within through the Mystery of the Unknown, we may find our Source, the Silent Spring from which all is born.

This journey from noise and confusion to Silent Being is not in any way an easy one, and not one which will be carried to the end by those that desire only ease and bodily peace. If you think you will breeze through the Gates of Silence with no trouble, then test yourself by spending a good length of time alone, in the dead quiet. Listen to your thought, and feel your heart. What do you hear and see, truly? If there is fear and ambition, desire and anxiety, your journey into Silence has just begun.

### Doubt Transports You
### by Abu Hamid al-Ghazali (1058-1111)

Doubt transports you to the truth. Who does not doubt fails to inquire. Who does not inquire fails to gain insight. Without insight, you remain blind and perplexed.

## *Concerning Asceticism, by Franklin Merrell-Wolff*

Throughout the history of religion, asceticism has played a highly important part, both as an enjoined discipline and as a spontaneously accepted practice. Several reasons underlie such practices, many of which have been listed and discussed by William James in his "Varieties of Religious Experience." However, I shall add certain considerations relative to this subject that have grown out of my personal experience and reflection.

I am convinced that for most natures and perhaps for all, a certain degree of ascetic practice is necessary if the individual is to attain his highest possibilities. But while this is particularly true with respect to preparing the Way for the Awakening, the same principle applies none the less in the unfolding or developing of power or skill in any field whatsoever. Man wins power in any direction by concentration of effort in the appropriate sense, but this involves inevitably a suppression of diffused activity. Combined with the main interest at any given time, most men feel within themselves counter interests and desires, and if the latter are indulged, the former are sacrificed. Here is a sufficient basis for essentially ascetic practice which may in extreme cases have all the value of the mortifications characteristic of some of the religious disciplines. A man may do this for the mastery of an art, of a science, for the building of a business, etc., just as well as for an objective of the type more commonly classified as religious. If the main interest is so all-consuming that there hardly remains any conflicting interest or desire, it may well be that but little discomfort is felt in the practice. On the other hand, important competing interests may cause the discipline to have the effect of real hardship. But, in any case, mastery in any field does require such discipline.

In the foregoing type of asceticism, there is no question of the essential sinfulness of the carnal nature. In fact, a rationale of asceticism may be developed entirely apart from the question of sin. Sin has been given a far too important place in religious thought and feeling. Such sin as there may be is largely incidental and the result of Ignorance and thus fundamentally a delusion rather than an actuality. The result of giving to sin the respect and attention which underlies the idea that it is of sufficient importance to be a worthy object of warfare is that sin is actually given life and power. *We never destroy anything by fighting it.*

A force that we fight may be temporarily crushed, because at the time we may be wielding a stronger force. But it remains true that we have won at the price of a certain exhaustion, and meanwhile the opposing force rebuilds itself, partly out of the very force we have expended. Then it comes back upon us when we are weak and may conquer us. No man escapes the action of this law simply by dying physically before the rebound. Somewhere he will live again, and in the next life he may find himself as much identified with evil as in the preceding life he thought himself to be identified with good.

Undoubtedly a strong carnal nature does have to be restrained, and in the case of those who do not have a sufficient balance-wheel of wisdom, possibly extreme effort in restraint may be necessary for a time. But unquestionably, it is far better if this discipline is looked upon in the rational spirit of regarding it as simply a form of training. The problem is vastly simplified if the individual, instead of taking an attitude of fighting or suppressing, will undertake to transmute the carnal energy. Every form of energy regardless of how seemingly evil it may be, has its higher mode or aspect into which it can be transformed. If the effort is focused upon this transforming, the energy is released and becomes a positive power, and this is relatively easy to do.

But after all is said and done, asceticism related to the carnal nature belongs only to the kindergarten stage of the training for the Higher Life of man. The higher and genuinely adult asceticisms are of an entirely different nature. Thus, when a man learns to become detached with respect to his pet opinions or ideas, and is willing to accept conclusions quite counter to his preferences when either evidence or logic points that way, then he is practicing asceticism in a higher and nobler sense. This kind of asceticism does cut far deeper into the real vitals of a man than any restraint connected with the mere carnal nature, and if he can succeed in the higher discipline, then anything remaining in the lesser nature requiring to be purified becomes a mere detail. In the superior discipline, the will has become so highly developed that the carnal nature is controlled relatively easily, provided the effort is put forth.

I would reduce the whole problem of asceticism to the following simple formula: *Let the individual concentrate his effort upon that which he desires most and restrain or transform incompatible desires.* What a man desires most may change as there is growth toward maturity. One implication of the formula, then, is to drop action in the direction of the old desire when the new and more potent desire takes its place. Of course, discrimination must be made between a persistent new desire and the mere temporary uprising of an inferior desire. The rule is to be applied as indicated only in the former case. This course followed consistently will achieve for the individual ultimately his highest good, and sooner or later that will mean the Awakened Consciousness. The advantage in this form of discipline lies largely in the fact that the center of emphasis is placed upon the positive value to be achieved, rather than upon the negative or interfering quality. It makes for a life of greater happiness, and this, in turn, arouses a greater strength, all of which means that success will come the more quickly, at least as a rule. Of course, such a policy of life practice may very well involve one or more radical changes of direction in the life activity. Thus a man may start his adult life with a desire to attain a great business success, but after having only partly completed this work, he may find that a greater desire takes its place. In that case, he might have to forego great success in the business sense and, remaining content with but moderate achievement in that field, throw the central focus of his energy in another direction. But while this would entail a smaller degree of success in the narrower field, the whole life of the individual, considered in the wider sense, would be more successful. Such a one would escape the tragedy of so many retired business men who, after leaving their businesses, find themselves quite helpless in a meaningless and barren life. From the standpoint of the Awakened Consciousness, all life here below is of value only in the sense of training for the Higher Life and has nothing in it that is valuable as an end-in-itself. So, from the higher point of view, the judgment of what constitutes success in the subject-object field is formed on quite a different basis from that of the usual world-standard. Everything here below is instrumental and only instrumental. So a life encompassing many but partial successes in the subject-object field may actually be making more progress toward the Awakening than a life which is highly successful in one concentrated field. From the higher standpoint, this lower life may be viewed in much the way a music-master views his pupil. The music-master has in mind finished perfection as the ultimate, but in the work-shop of the studio the time is given almost wholly to fragments, such as the technical handling of a phrase, the building of tone-quality, etc. This life here is such a studio and only that. The concert stage is Cosmic Consciousness.

Once a man has Awakened to the Higher Consciousness, he may make a decision that requires the very highest ascetic resolution. He Knows the infinite superiority of the Higher Life in every sense, and, if he had only himself individually to consider, naturally he would choose that Higher Life exclusively. But consideration for the needs of others may lead him to forego this and accept a life in the world while, at the same time, it is not a life of the world. As a part of his work, he may move rather freely in the field of sensation, emotion, etc., and may even seem self-indulgent to the superficial observer, yet all the while he would be practicing asceticism in the severest sense in the very living in that way. For him there is not any longer a question of resisting carnal temptation, for Knowledge of the higher Joy has reduced all this to husks and ashes, relatively speaking. He simply endures what the carnal man imagines to be enjoyment.

The whole problem of asceticism appears to me, from my present perspective, as merely one of rational judgment and wisdom and is quite divorced from the emotional unpleasantness that is usually associated with it. It is simply good sense to choose the greater value in any conflict of values. Why should this be regarded as an occasion for serious emotional stress?

Start each day with a smile and get it over with. ~ *W.C. Fields*

Responsibility, n. A detachable burden easily shifted to the shoulders of God, Fate, Fortune, Luck, or one's neighbor. In the days of astrology it was customary to unload it upon a star. ~ *Ambrose Bierce*

I have great faith in fools; self-confidence my friends call it. ~ *Edgar Allan Poe*

Put your hand on a hot stove for a minute, and it seems like an hour. Sit with a pretty girl for an hour, and it seems like a minute. THAT'S relativity. ~ *Albert Einstein, as "quoted" by Steve Mirsky*

The only people who rejoice at births and mourn at funerals are the parties that aren't involved. ~ *Mark Twain*

# 4: The Thinker and the Feeler

*How I Came to Understand then Overcome Autism
Conditions ... from the Inside Out, by Steve Brier*

I overcame most, if not all, Asperger and other savant-like autism symptoms as an adult taking a decade and a half of 24/7 efforts. Rote speech, lack of coordination, ritual behaviors, lack of color vision and depth perception, so-called mind blindness (I call these "cosmic conniptions") and more were overcome....

Language was last to come. I became completely fluent in normal speech where words have normal meaning *in the last two years*. I did this after getting no help for seven fruitless years from fancy, expensive, and highly regarded New York City talk therapists.

How can a lone individual understand and overcome [what authorities and institutions haven't]? ... They looked *out*. I looked *in*....

I used intuition…. While scientific methods were used to obtain information and data to understand what was happening to me, spiritual means were used to overcome and solve challenges….

What was I observing? Anything that looked and felt like my experience, thoughts, behavior, dreams, speech, all….

Assuming I found real workable insights, would that alone change my Asperger genes, my birth delivery injuries made worse by abysmal upbringing? The answer was a resounding yes. I found if I honestly observed patterns of my behavior and then correlated them to dreams, dream images, or objective patterns in nature, my behaviors would dissolve over time. I only had to be honest and trust intuition.

I would not be able to trust feelings, sensations, even brain functions because they would take time to heal. I found my behavior, no matter how strange, was meaningful, purposeful, attempting from an unseen part of myself to express something that didn't have words. I knew if I externalized my disabilities, then I could see them. If I could see them, then I could heal them. If I could heal them, maybe, just maybe, I could make me a whole person….

### *Poems by Shawn Nevins*

Between thought and thought
are such lonely spaces
that we may lose hold of our selves.
Such fears grip those who cannot sit still.
To be lost is the prelude to discovery.
To be afraid is to approach knowledge.

Can you hear my silence,
or do you chatter incessantly?
Each word is backed by Nothingness.
A well absorbing echoes.
Listen to me —
Stillness between your every word.

Beyond rightness,
What is Reality?
The mind grasps perfection,
But what is an Eternity?
Beyond the balance of life and death,
Beyond the mind, bursting thought.
"Nothing to cling to or stay your fall."

This black wall within my mind,
ancient river of Styx reborn,
waters of mystery, unknowing,
silently challenging my life for its meaning.
Again and again I join ranks
turning within upon the limits of my self
asking "what?" "who?" "is?"

Now, looking within,
the waters rush through my bones
and the darkness looks upon itself
knowing that it is
and all else is not.

Breeze,
you are always ready for today,
for this moment.
Exhaled from a place of quiet
to rattle this world
and bare the words from our thoughts
for your message,
whispered inside our lives,
of what was, could be, and is.

I ask nothing with words.
My look says all —

Everything is a burning bush.
I look with your eyes
Upon Nothing.
Everyone looks with the eyes of the Other,
For all are dispossessed.

"Cat Confrontation"

She thinks I'm a ghost,
this feline accuser
eyeing me warily
with a one-paw advance.
Uncanny, how she looks to each side,
then right through me.

She may be right.
I suspect I've been here before,
yet am not sure I'm here now.
Is all the world a wraith,
or am I
neither here nor there
drifting somehow
between?

Would we see light without its shadow,
without its particulate partner
lending it form?
The blind sun sees
none of this;
*is* all of this.

## *Three Questions, by Art Ticknor*

What are you able to see by introspection? For the person seeking self-knowledge, the distinction between subject and object, between viewer and view, is critical. And the view needs to include what we generally consider interior territory. But when we observe the mind, we often find ourselves going round and round in whirlpool-like circles. So the question arises of whether there is a certain progression of focus that may help. I think there is and that it can be represented by a series of questions that the introspector can ask himself.

*Question 1: Are you the thinker, the feeler?*

Are you able to watch thoughts and feelings with detachment? If not, an "effortless" meditation (see the December 2005 TAT Forum for a description by Mike Conners) or vipassana technique may be useful. The key to a dispassionate observing of thoughts may be a certain inner relaxation that gives us a degree of freedom from being identified with them. I'm using the term "thought" in a broad sense to include the ever-changing series of images flickering on the screen of awareness, including mentation and feelings as well as what we generally suppose to be the outside world—all objects of awareness.

I realize I may be skipping blithely over something that's a stumbling block for many of us, which is watching feelings with the same detachment as we're able to summon for watching thoughts. For the emotional seeker, identification with feelings is the seeming life-blood of existence ("I might as well be dead as have no feelings"). It's not a question of having no feelings but of not being identified with them, of realizing that they are parts of the scenery, not parts of the viewer. For the intellectual seeker, feelings are irrational and therefore somewhat of an embarrassment as well as threatening—clues to their unacknowledged importance in our self-belief.

If you are able to watch thoughts, where do they come from? Are you selecting which thoughts to have? Do you create your thoughts by premeditated choice? Or do thoughts happen to you, coming into consciousness—including dream consciousness—without your making them? Are you the thinker, or are you experiencing thought? If you're not sure, keep looking until you are.

*Question 2: Are you the decision-maker, the doer?*

Once you see the truth about the first question, then it's time to take the next step inward. This involves an expansion of the view to include mental processes such as decision-making. Just as you don't know where the switch is to allow the objective observation of thoughts, you don't know how to switch your focus to get behind the decision-making process. These inward steps occur by seeming accident but are propelled by effort. By considering the results of decisions and wondering about why they came out the way they did, by keeping alert to the inner conflicts that occupy a good part of our interior scenery, watching the ongoing arguments without trying to interfere in the process, an accident may occur sooner or later, and you'll see the decision-making process itself from an anterior point of observation.

In my case, I witnessed the decision-making process operating in slow-motion at a time of high tension—like the slow-motion witnessing that often happens to people who realize they're about to experience a car crash. But inner seeing doesn't necessarily have a visual feel to it. More generally it's an intuitive seeing, as in: "Oh, now I see what you mean." In other words, something has become intuitively obvious to us.

As with the first question, look until you see clearly what your role is in the decision-making process. Are you the decision-maker, determining which inner conflicts will arise at what times, orchestrating the courtroom procedure as judge and jury? Are you then the "doer" who carries out the decisions that you, in your role of judge and jury, have made? Or are you the awareness that is observing the inner argument, the decision-making, and the resultant doing?

The greatest miracle of existence is the impossibility of existence itself. (How did the first thing arise out of nothing?) Miracles affecting physical manifestation are the lowest level of amazements. Between these two extremes are the miracles that occur as the mind's processes come into conscious view. And when that occurs, your conviction of being in control, of being in the driver's seat, may run into overwhelming data to the contrary. Your belief that if you "let go" and just let things take their own course your life would fall apart at the seams may be based on a delusion of control—like the child whose car seat has a steering wheel, which he uses to steer the car.

*Question 3: Who or what is observing?*

The path to self-knowledge has two broad avenues, one being the route of bhakti or devotion and the other the path of jnana or self-inquiry.

The devotee hopes to lose himself in the object of his worship, while the self-inquirer hopes to find himself through direct seeing or wisdom. The process of questioning the self by observation probably appeals more to the latter than the former. True knowledge or wisdom comes through knowing what you're not, but the two categories of mentality approach this in different ways.

The self-inquirer knows that to find the self he has to distinguish self from not-self. Faulty identification with the not-self is what prevents true self-knowing. The self, the subject, is the observer. Everything that comes into the view is an object of observation—and therefore not-self.

We can, through Douglas Harding's experiments for example, glimpse what we're looking out from. And of course what we're looking out from is the us that's aware, isn't it. But then the contradiction arises between the conviction that what we're looking out from is Awareness and the conviction that I'm a separate something observing (i.e., aware of) Awareness. Do we own a personal awareness, each of us grasping his own separate "mind," scared to death that disease or death will destroy that prize possession?

There is only one Awareness. God, the Source, the Real Self— whatever you want to call it—is the eye that sees itself. To know the Self is not a perceptual or a conceptual knowing but, as Franklin Merrell-Wolff stated, a knowing by identity. We recognize our Self when the false identities drop off. That is also where the paths of losing the self and finding the self meet.

### Go Deeper than Love, by D.H. Lawrence
### from Know Deeply, Know Thyself More Deeply

Go deeper than love, for the soul has greater depths,
love is like the grass, but the heart is deep wild rock
molten, yet dense and permanent.

Go down to your deep old heart, and lose sight of yourself.
And lose sight of me, the me whom you turbulently loved.
Let us lose sight of ourselves, and break the mirrors.
For the fierce curve of our lives is moving again to the depths
out of sight, in the deep living heart.

*Living in the Now? by Bob Cergol*

Some say in order to hear the silence or to abide in stillness you simply need to focus your attention on the present, "be" in the "now." Various techniques are offered for achieving this. But is this really possible? Can you actually do this? Have you ever actually done this? Does this mean focusing your attention so keenly on sensory perceptions that the "you" having those perceptions is momentarily forgotten? Does it mean that you visualize the way you imagine that you should feel if you were "living in the now"? If so, then all you are doing is holding on to one thought for whatever the duration of your experience of "now" was—merely forgetting that the identity-based, body/mind "you" still surrounds that experience. (Identity still spins identity.) This isn't living in the now, it's living in the past—waiting for the future to fulfill that past thought. It is spinning, after the fact, the stream of consciousness into an experience that belonged to you. You did not observe the observer. You only invented or witnessed an experience. You did not transcend the ego-self. Forgetfulness of self is not the same as self-transcendence, and it is possible that for a lot of people these meditation techniques merely induce a state of self-forgetfulness, which is then interpreted as some profound experience. It is just that, a pleasant experience. The "you" you take yourself to be cannot exist in the present moment. Recognition of one's true nature is beyond time—and one's attempts to hold one's attention in a particular point in time, conceived as "now," is an exercise in self-hypnosis. It is by witnessing experience—not participating in it—that one discovers what one is not. Focusing the attention in such a way as to create an experience is exactly the opposite of what is required. The real "you" is the timeless, present presence—and the recognition of such places both time and self "out there" as phenomena witnessed.

### The Joke's on Lin-chi

*The earliest record of ch'an Buddhist illumination experiences, The Transmission of the Lamp, contains the following story:*

Lin-chi, after his awakening, remained for a time with Huang-po. One day Lin-chi went with Huang-po to do some work, in which all the monks participated. Lin-chi followed his master, who, turning his head, noticed that Lin-chi was carrying nothing in his hand.

"Where is your hoe?"

"Somebody took it away."

"Come here, let's talk," Huang-po commanded, and as Lin-chi drew nearer, Huang-po thrust his hoe into the ground and said, "There is no one in the world who can pick up my hoe."

Lin-chi seized the tool, lifted it and exclaimed, "How then could it be in my hands?"

"Today we have another hand with us. It is not necessary for me to join in."

And Huang-po returned to the temple.

# 5: The Original State

## On Effective Teaching, by Bob Cergol

I am moving toward the opinion that all the inspiring stuff—Rumi, Nisargadatta, etc.—while valuable and having its time and place, largely induces sleep—just the opposite of what the authors would hope for. It has value when used in small doses by someone to cultivate the feeling side of those overly-intellectual, egocentric readers. Beyond that it is soporific and a tool for the ego to look away—and imbibe the mood—not to look at self. For a person in the right position it could be a trigger, but that would be rare, and I am increasingly convinced that it is not even going to move someone to that position where some trigger could be effective.

I am increasingly coming to conclude that what a teacher must do is stimulate distress in the student by attacking the objects on which they are focused in their lives, i.e., attack the life, whatever it is that they are living, to create doubt and consternation. (Of course this can't be totally indiscriminate.) In that state the inner essence will then have the possibility of being listened to—and the poem's meaning might penetrate and be effective. Rose was always "attacking" the world—our world—that we lived in. We all thought it was a reflection of his idiosyncrasies. Not at all, it was a reflection of his understanding that to move the mind to the position it might be in if it were confronted with death, he had to attack all of the things that it was focused upon—lost in. Inertia and gravity do not go in this direction. Minds do not drift into the state of being at the "end-of-their-rope." Nisargadatta does not accomplish this with his lullabies of eternality, nor does Rumi. The time to listen to the lullaby is when the panic-stricken mind needs a rest—but an inspiring rest of the poetry of the eternal, not tension-relieving dissipation.

The reason to attack the life someone is living is to pry them loose from it prematurely, i.e., before their physical death. If someone is lucky enough, as my father was, to be given a scheduled death sentence (cancer) and also be in a position to think about one's life, then they will simultaneously accept the life that was lived and is being lived—after all it's a *fait accompli*—but they will look at it as utterly unimportant, or certainly from a more distant perspective. It is that sort of attitude that can result in the attention turning in on itself instead of being so fixated outwardly on the dream. Death being the end-of-the-road, with no escape as a backdrop, can make it possible to simply look at life without defensiveness, without argument, and see what is there, what is really going on. That viewing can start a chain reaction. The prospect of impending death has the power to propel the mind into a state of between-ness. Rose—the true Zen master—was doing just that with his incessant confronting of his students about the life they were living and the world in which they [thought they] were living.

## *Poems by Shawn Nevins*

Caught between this vision and the next,
I am a shadow blown by the wind.
I am moving light,
quiet that vibrates,
a pulse between each beat.

I am suggestions of eternity
in the overlooked corners of dreams.
I am always waiting
for those who are thankful for each day
and care not if they see the end.

               ❦

"City Morning"

Water flows as asphalt
bending and curving through curbs
like channels between multistory hills of steel.
What is a tree other than a street lamp,
and a bird but a scrap of paper
fluttering?
Ferns become fire hydrants
and two-legged deer browse
in coffee shops by stone tables.
Street light, car light, office light, flashing light,
every one a star;
every one a dewdrop on broken glass.
My watch says 6 AM.
All is a picture.
All is perfect.
It is morning everywhere.

               ❦

Close your eyes
to what you were.
Relax.
Let the shimmering strands of self
part in a dream-like breeze of not-caring.
The answer is here.
Home is here.
Waiting.

Clouds curtain open
and waters dance
with mirrored light advancing and retreating
across time.
All manner of life and death
flows with this river,
yet the sound remains the same —
an eternal, immutable pause
between....

There's a cold wind coming down
that shakes a man to the ground.
There's a cold wind coming down
that makes him think and makes him frown,
and makes him hear every sound.

There's a cold wind coming down
that calls his name out from the crowd,
yet calls the name of every child,
follows him every mile,
speaks to him without a smile,
takes from him all trace of guile.

There's a cold wind coming down
to relieve him of thoughts of gain,
free him from fortune's pain,
and force him from these lonely chains.

Come deeper with me
to the place of watchers of watching.
To the place where all becomes shadow.
Where our lacy mind blows in a gentle breeze
that is the whispering breath of God.
A god who gently laughs as he himself
slips under waters as still as death.

Leave me and you will find me.
Within and behind is the Golden Find.

For the first time
I feel the comfort of dissolution,
the restful end of knowledge,
and the security of nothing to hold on to.

The certainty of that which never changes
brings a smile to this that changes every day.

A new life with no baggage.
Crossing the border a free man.
Beyond all wanting and needing
is the ceasing of being that belongs to all.

"The world is an illusion."
So saying, the Zen master rises from his seat —
Swats a mosquito on his forehead.

## *Wheel of Manifestations, by Gary Harmon*

In the original state, sometimes known as the original face, bound-less awareness dwells. This is I Am or I Exist, without any memory, understanding or conditioning, without attributes, without structure or identity. Nothing is separate from the entirety. This is the state of pure unmanifested awareness.

Then, for no apparent explanation (other than that Its nature to do so), arises the thought or conception, I Am, the impersonal at-tentiveness, on which the world appears as a holo-matrix. This is the source of duality. A womb is found in which to grow.

Consciousness, in order to manifest itself, needs a shape, a material shell, which it identifies as itself and thus starts the concept of "bond-age," with an imaginary objectification of "I." Whenever one thinks and acts from the standpoint of this self-identification, one could be said to have committed the "original sin" of turning pure subjectivity of the immeasurable potential into an object, a limited actuality. This is the birth of duality, a separate existence from all other perceived objects.

No object has, or can have, a self-sufficient existence of its own. An object cannot awaken itself from another object. The holo-matrix phantom individual, which is now a supposed object, is seeking another object, the "Absolute" or "Reality" or whatever.

If this is clear, one must reverse 180 degrees, turn around and go back to find out what one originally was (and always has been) before consciousness occurred.

At this stage comes the "awakening." One is neither the body, nor even the consciousness, but the unnamable condition of total, unmanifested potentiality. Prior to the arrival of consciousness. The seeker disappears in the seeking. When the seeker disappears, there is no question of doing. This body is perceptible, but our true nature is that which was before the body and the consciousness came into being. Anything that is sensually seen and interpreted by the mind is an appearance in consciousness and is not true, for it is temporal.

And so the cycle is complete; the seeker and what is sought are the same. The seeker is the sought. This is the state of pure unmanifested awareness. This is the spot where we started our expedition from.

### *Always Right Behind You*
### *by Art Ticknor*

*I am always right behind you*
But turn around and you won't see me.
I am never not with you —
Why aren't you always with me?
I am at the center
while you stay at the periphery.
I am there, too,
but you won't find me there.
When you turn round
the center stays behind you.
Stand still while turning your gaze around
and look at what you're looking out of.

### Tricks, by Bob Fergeson

As individual points of awareness, our chief feature is one of identifying. We become whatever we stare at long enough, and we have been looking at the body/mind since birth. This hypnosis is so strong, most of us cannot escape it without help. The ego, being the clever, self-righteous fool that it is, will not let us accept this help, so we have to be tricked. Fortunately, the Powers That Be invented some very useful tricks to help us out. All tricks are for destroying the ego-centric fantasy that we actually exist, as the body/mind or anything else for that matter, and for freeing us from believing that there is such a thing as an individual "self." They serve to back the awareness out of the individual mind/memory and into the state of universal awareness, away from self into silent witness. Thus, a retreat or dis-identification from the mind and its projections is caused, hopefully leading to the realization of one's true self: the observer. Here are a few tricks to get you going but remember … they won't work if you actually believe any of this.

**Trick of going against negative emotions:** This helps lead us away from the extreme defensiveness of the egocentric position. We believe we're doing good and being virtuous by not being negative, but we are actually just moving away from manically defending the false or particular, i.e. the "self." This brings about an inner movement towards a more universal view where one thing, or self, is not set up against another. This trick is also known as "helping others," practicing virtues, etc.

**Trick of "know thyself:"** The point of this trick is to cause disidentification with the individual memory pattern by becoming familiar with it: what we see is not us. Getting to know the robot leads, hopefully, to realizing it's not you. The information gained by knowing one's self isn't the point, it's the inner movement or retreat that counts. So, don't worry if you discover you're not the person you thought you were.

**Trick of effortless meditation:** We simply watch our thoughts without being attached or affected. Again, we're led within, as this trick serves to unattach us from our personal reactive mind and places us in the universal rather than the particular. This trick has the added benefit of being quite peaceful.

**Trick of self-remembering, "Who Am I?" meaningless Zen koans, etc.:** These tricks are quite simple, and therefore very effective. The ego loves complexity and distraction, so the act of focusing the attention on an unanswerable, meaningless koan knocks the ego off its feet, for a bit. Eventually, we may become less afraid of the silent unknown. The movement back and forth between the formal (mind chatter) and informal (silent awareness following the shock of perplexity) might bring about a triangulation: the body/mind and accompanying "self" or looker may be seen for what they are.

**Trick of self-inquiry:** Great trick for the astute, since they think they'll have it figured out in no time. Eventually, they might come to find they're not as clever as they thought. It can lead the inquirer to accidentally going within, thus being effective. At its best, it will cause a surrender, or ego-death, when the mind comes to a dead end, thus teaming up with the trick below.

**Trick of surrender:** A most powerful trick in that we are led to believe we are doing something pious, and instead end up getting a good look at our pride. The trick is that we've never been in charge anyway, meaning we do nothing and never have. Surrender as an act of the prideful, pious ego usually fails miserably. This can eventually lead us to inquire as to what we did wrong, thus leading us back to the trick above. If both inquiry and surrender are practiced, we might trick ourselves right into a massive ego-death, so be careful ... don't get tricked.

STANLEY WAS DEEPLY DISAPPOINTED WHEN, HIGH IN THE TIBETAN MOUNTAINS, HE FINALLY FOUND HIS TRUE SELF.

# 6: SELF-HONESTY

## Persistence & Self-Honesty, by Shawn Nevins

I am not outstanding in any quality. Yet, I attained a spiritual realization, so there is hope for others. In examining my decade of seeking, I think the qualities of persistence and self-honesty proved key.

Persistence implies desire, but I never felt I wanted the Truth badly enough. I always felt short of my ideal seeker who asked every waking moment, "Who am I?" I never felt driven. Perhaps that is a result of my biology. I am more of a long-distance walker than runner or sprinter. The walker may not show sweat on the brow, yet be just as driven as the runner.

Mr. Rose once said, "If I tell you to go five miles, don't walk a mile then turn back." Though I certainly fell to the ground many times, I always got up and kept walking. Why? Because I knew, in my heart, that there was NOTHING ELSE TO DO. This is where the self-honesty comes into play. Think through your desires and see where they take you.

Other than the spiritual search, I believe my strongest desire was to retreat to a cabin in the woods. It was a nostalgic dream of a perpetual summer evening complete with front porch swing, a dog, and sweet iced tea. Yet, I knew that moment of perfection would never last. I also knew that I had limited energy in life. I could choose the cabin—the known but ultimately hollow—or choose the unknown but potentially complete spiritual search. For me, every dream ended in death, and the discovery of my true nature seemed the only hope of escape.

Self-honesty is developed. For this, I see the value of my years of character development while with the SKS. If you learn to see your daily lies, you will learn to see the larger lies. You must find a point within your self from which you can judge the garbage from lesser garbage. A teacher helps in this respect. Around him, you may sense his perspective and see clearly the idiocy of your daily pursuits. Books, being in nature, music, meditation, friends, many things may give you a truer perspective. You will know it when you find it. One really does back away from untruth. Until, finally, your momentum is in one direction and you no longer care—you just want to know the Truth.

This was all done in tiny steps and nowhere along the way did I feel, "Aha! Now I am a seeker, now I am a vector, now I am one hundred percent committed." I think that was a good thing. When one feels they are falling short, they are probably working as hard as they can, and when they feel they are at their maximum, they probably have more to give.

More important than a specific, verbal commitment to find the Truth, is the action of self-honesty. As Rose would say, "Tell the truth in all things relative." If you are honest, you will realize that you don't know anything for certain. That uncertainty will haunt you and keep you moving. You hide from the uncertainty by distractions, but it is always in the back of your mind.

Lest you get the idea that I was a paragon of persistence and self-honesty, I will point out that several times I threw up my hands in despair and fatigue. The worst of these was early in 1998, when I decided that I was finished with seeking and would go make a fortune instead. Perhaps everyone hits a point where they convince themselves that they cannot attain—that the task is too great. Sometimes, the mind simply loses interest in the search. I have no easy answer for these dark times, except that in each instance, something appeared which reignited my interest. Being surrounded by fellow seekers helped. It is as if one is delirious and needs friends to watch over them until they recover. Unfortunately, in their delirium, they see their friends as enemies and try to flee. "To the sick man, sweet water tastes bitter."

Let's say a boat goes down miles from shore. There are some people who, floating in the water, decide they will never make it to shore and give up on the spot. These people don't begin a spiritual path. Others point in the direction of shore and start swimming, confident they will make it. These people soon discover if they are truly courageous or not. Finally, some say they cannot make it, but start swimming anyway. These are the most courageous. They have learned to act in the face of despair.

We back away from untruth and judge the untrue from a higher perspective. The higher perspective is eventually judged from another, superior perspective. Until the end, I was never certain of anything. I think that is the value of Rose's emphasis on using reason and intuition. For me, one perpetually doubted the other, so I kept striving for a superior state—a state of certainty.

I was not a born seeker. My plans for the perfect life were trounced and in the resulting state of despair I felt the emptiness of life. The despair was born of an honest appraisal of my situation. I stumbled upon a lecture by Mr. Rose, and for the first time realized the possibility of discovering the meaning of life. I was twenty-two years old before I read my first spiritual book. At first, the spiritual search substituted for other failed pursuits and propped up my wounded ego. I suppose I could have rested in the conceit that I was a spiritual seeker and superior to my fellows, but I did not. Perhaps it was the sense I got from Mr. Rose that there was something ultimate to be discovered. That sense of the ultimate is the most important thing to communicate. Once you have had a taste, it will haunt you.

Again I return to self-honesty. You know that there is more than the way you are living. You have a superior perspective, yet you chose to forget. You cannot escape. You are simply running in circles. Persistence is a natural outcome of honesty. Commitment is the fruit of honesty.

Honesty may very well bring despair, then you must have faith. Faith born of your own contact with the edges of the Ultimate or in the knowledge that others have attained. Know that the path of honesty will lead you through the final despair—through death itself.

## *The Little Man, by Bob Fergeson*

From early morning coffee
to late night herbal tea,
We lived for near forever,
the Little Man and me.

When first I came to travel
in this classroom wide and grand,
I knew nothing of the coming
of this lonely Little Man.

But parents, teachers, doctors,
the whole damn Helping Herd,
soon created him inside me,
as their ancestors had insured.
He has no real existence,
none that I can see.
But could and should and would!
screamed the Little Man in me.

Soon I hid myself in pride,
found that fear blocked every door.
I was now what I despised!
just as those that'd gone before.

The hypnosis worked it's magic,
no peace had I, no stand.
Just a mis-identification,
I became the Little Man.
I took him for a person,
Hell, I thought that he was me!
He sure could be convincing,
that Little Man in me.

Then one day it happened,
I know not really why.
I looked out there below me
from some Great Eternal Sky.
He didn't even notice,
so busy as a bee,
He just kept right on sleeping, but
That Little Man ain't me!

One day looking in the mirror,
as I got up from the can,
I receded back behind him,
that sleeping Little Man.
He didn't even notice,
just a grain lost in the sand.
He can't look back and see me,
that lonely Little Man.

I watch him and his pattern,
how he blends right in so well,
that his life and his surroundings
are no different from himself.
He has no greater vision,
desire and fear are all he sees.
An actor in the TV,
that Little Man in me.

It's a sad, but true short story,
I cry a tear, and so does he,
He won't survive, he lives to die,
the Little Man in me.

## *Things Are Not What They Seem, by Bart Marshall*

Dreams have long been used as a metaphor for the transient, ephemeral, un-real nature of waking life. Plato used the analogy of shadows cast on a cave wall by firelight. Contemporary philosophers have compared waking life to a movie projected on a screen. Now we can create metaphors from holograms and virtual reality. But they all convey the same message: "Things are not what they seem."

These metaphors also ask: "Who is it that watches this dream/ shadow/movie/game?" Where is the observer behind it all that ISN'T a shadow character in the dream? Right now, for instance, is it the observer who reads these words? Is it the one who stands apart in judgment of the reader? Is it some ultimate observer you believe in but have yet to touch? Or is it perhaps that as deep into the observer lineup as we go in this hall of mirrors the observers are all false?

In the end, it seems, there is no real observer behind it all. There is no place of final refuge. It is always the same false observer, slipping into a new guise as an anterior, superior, observer. Observers, no matter how sublime, must by their very nature stand apart from what is observed or they cease to be. In Reality, nothing stands apart. There is only Unity, the One.

It is the dream of an ultimate observer—a place of final refuge— that blocks the light. When observing stops, the Real appears—crystal clear and empty.

## My Last Identity, by Irene Palmer

Here, in my last Identity
Having become all I will ever be
There is peace, a peace of finality.

Yet behind the threads of life
There is a prevailing presence
     of something left unsaid.

I listen to the silence of that faint voice
That hovers on the outer edge
     of darkness, There is no desire to become entangled
     in life's emotional threads again.

Ambition is laid to rest,
No desire to become someone, for fame,
To go to foreign cities, to see the world.
No harboring regrets of what I have done
     or didn't do,
No worry what might have been
     or yet might be.

The world is timeless.
     I am alone.

## The Ego, by Art Ticknor

The final, most obstinate, and most wily of all obstructions to crossing the finish line to Nirvana is the ego. The ego is not:

- Pride ("He's a proud fellow, struts around like a rooster").
- Selfishness ("She only thinks of herself").
- Narcissism ("He's in love with himself").
- Something to school, polish or perfect.
- Something to try to minimize or to kill off.

The ego is not a collection of our negative attributes. The ego does have a game it likes to play, though, splitting the personality patterns into two camps: the "good" ones that it identifies with (me, the saint, the angel) and the "bad" ones that it disowns (not me, the devil made me do it, the sinner).

The ego is a belief planted in us by what created us—a belief that we're something (some thing).

The ego is the individuality-sense itself. It is the "I am" that identifies with certain forms, feelings and constructs:

- I am hungry.
- I am the guy in the mirror.
- I am the person who wakes in the morning and falls asleep at night.
- I am unhappy.
- I am the person who was born a certain number of years ago and will die at some uncertain time in the future.
- I am the person with this name and this set of personality traits and memories that make me unique.
- I am lovable.
- I am the individual body-mind that is separate from other body-minds and whose existence is threatened and subject to extinction.
- I am the spirit or soul that will survive the death of the body.

We view our life-experience through the sense-of-self. It is the innermost observer that we're identified with and is thus not something that comes into our view. So how can we observe it?

Richard Rose has the most practical, common-sense system for bringing this about that I've come across. The general outline is one of retreating from false identification (a process which Merrell-Wolff also touched on in his "Induction" talk). It's not a logical process that can be conducted by analysis or argument but a process of introspective observation. A sample progression might go something like this:

- I *have* a body—which implies that it's not the innermost me.
- Similarly, I have thoughts and feelings—admittedly more interior possessions than my shirt and shoes, but still not me.
- I can scrutinize the beliefs and convictions that run my life, thus putting them more consciously into my view, where I realize they, too, are possessions (or obsessions).
- I can view my decision-making process—first indirectly, by looking at the results, and then directly—seeing that this process is part of the mind's automatic machinery that functions regardless of whether I'm aware of watching it or not. I see that I'm not "the decider," and yet I insist that I'm the final arbiter.

- ♦ I can see that I'm not "the doer," since action results from thought, which has already happened when I become aware of it. Yet despite lack of control, I try to be in control. After all, what would happen if I just gave up?
- ♦ I can view and review my defensive reactions when I feel threatened—anger, sarcasm, lashing out, withdrawal, arguing, feeling superior, feeling hurt, shocked, rejected, looking for comfort, replaying events in my imagination and having them come out differently, planning revenge, etc. These threats are afflictions to the individuality-sense and therefore clues to its existence and whereabouts.
- ♦ As Merrell-Wolff sums it up: "I'm not the mind, I'm not the feelings, I'm not the body—that I see. But I surely *am*, I surely am an individual, apart from others."

This sense of being something apart is the ego. Eventually there is a direct seeing into what we're looking out from and a realization that the only observer is the Observatory.

To err is human—but it feels divine. ~ *Mae West*

Never eat more than you can lift. ~ *Miss Piggy*

It's better to remain quiet and let people think you are a fool than to open your mouth and remove all doubt. ~ *Lincoln*

April 1: This is the day upon which we are reminded of what we are on the other three hundred and sixty-four. ~ *Mark Twain*

Real friends are those who upon watching you make a fool of yourself do not feel that the job was done permanently. ~ *Anonymous*

# 7: Listening

## *Finding the Way, by Franklin Merrell-Wolff*

Much that I have written in this book [*Pathways Through to Space*] is in the form of an intimate personal testimony. Other portions are in the form of reflective discussions, or more or less mystical compositions that are, in large measure at least, the fruit of a shift in consciousness level which I, individually, have experienced. My purpose in this was not merely the satisfying of a demand for self-expression—in fact I do not feel such a demand—but to report and reveal, as far as may be, a fact that I know to be of the very highest importance to myself, and a fact that is potentially capable of having the same value for others. From previous training, I know something of the importance and technique of introspective self-observation. I have not neglected watching the personal transformation, while in process, with a view to keeping a record of as large an objective value as I could achieve. It has been my purpose not to neglect the recording of unpleasant or negative features if they should arise. In point of fact, I have found the unpleasant features to be of remarkably minor importance and only of temporary duration. Thus any ordinary athletic achievement in the field of sports involves more bodily and emotional discomfort than I have experienced at any time since the 7th of last month, while on the other hand I have known the Joy of finding a World far greater and far more significant than all that which came out of the discoveries of Columbus. I simply wish that others may find the World, or have the Way made clearer to them because of what I have already accomplished.

There is one point that I wish to have understood very clearly. The initial Transformation did not just happen to me as something coming unexpectedly out of the blue. We have several records of such spontaneous Awakenings, and while there exists a rationale explaining such cases which shows that they are not quite so spontaneous as they seem, I shall not enter into that question at the present time. In point of fact, I have sought this Awakening for several years. I was finally convinced that, at least in all probability, there was such a thing or event, while I was in the midst of the discussions of a metaphysical seminary held at Harvard. I saw, at once, that if such Knowledge were an actuality it was of far greater importance than even the greatest intellectual achievement within the limits of the subject-object field. At that time I had a very imperfect idea of the Goal, but I knew that among the East Indians was to be found the greatest development of knowledge relative to It. I resolved to make the search and pay what price might be demanded. In the years since, I have been more than once discouraged and have permitted lateral desires to lead me into side-excursions. But I always returned to the search. I tested various different routes, finding values and defects in all, and then at last by combining the best that India has to offer in the field of metaphysics with the best of western science and philosophy, and then adding thereto some modifications of my own,* I found a road that has proved successful. While during the interim there have been partial Transformations and Recognitions, it has taken twenty-four years of search to attain a culminating point which I can recognize as definitely culminating. All of the steps within the subject-object field were conscious, and therefore I can formulate and evaluate them. Also, I am aware of the Transcendent Factor and know the Significance of the part It plays. If I had known in the beginning all that is here for the first time collected together between the covers of one book, many years of time would have been saved. Perhaps, also, for some others this book may have a similar value. But from the standpoint of evidence for a Beyondness, the point I wish to make is that in the present case an individual was finally convinced of the validity of a search from the discussions that formed part of the classwork in one of the leading western universities. He tried to find the Way, at times following others, but in the end carving his own course, and did that without renouncing the western form of intellectuality. What one can do others also may do.

My final word on this particular subject is: I sought a Goal the existence of which I had become convinced was highly probable. I succeeded in finding this Goal, and now I KNOW, and can also say to all others: "IT IS ABSOLUTELY WORTH ANYTHING THAT IT MAY COST, AND IMMEASURABLY MORE."

* At the present time, some two and one-half years since writing the above, I have a further contribution to offer on the creative effort supplied by the individual himself. I have made many experiments with the meditative and yogic techniques given by the various authorities. In no case have I had any results that were worth the effort so long as I did not supply at least a self-devised modification of my own. Apparently the modification is suggested intuitively. Often I got results by a method diametrically opposite to that suggested by a given authority. At least, so far as my private experience is concerned, the successful method always had to be in some measure an original creation. I suspect the presence of a general principle here, but I am not at present able to deduce a conclusion of universal applicability.

### Rapport, by Art Ticknor

Would you like to feel love?
Raise the portcullis,
drop the drawbridge.
Love is within,
but we stay out.

Begin with fresh eyes:
see your friend for the first time.
The door is open.
At the center
you and the friend
are not two.

## The Listening Attention in Inquiry and Surrender
### by Bob Fergeson

*The following is not meant to imply there is "nothing to be done" or to be a shortcut or trick to release. It is not for the lazy or clever, but written for those who have spent perhaps years of disciplined work on themselves and their commitment to finding the Truth.*

To find that which lies beyond the mind, "the golden find," we must follow one of two paths. The first, and most familiar with the western mind, is the path of self-inquiry. The other is that of devotion or bhakti, the path of surrender. Both of these paths, if followed with earnestness, *but not effort*, can lead to realization. Let me explain.

The path of self-inquiry leads one to truth through discrimination and retreat. We see what we are not through unbiased observation, which leads us to un-attach ourselves from the false. It is not, and cannot be, a process of deciding what we will find and then going about creating or proving our theory. This is the state and practice of the ego, not of the truth.

Our mind has an almost infinite capacity to create, but little training in simple observation and questioning. To create is to do, to put forth effort. To simply observe, or to listen with the inner awareness, does not give the ego the central position it so craves. To observe or listen is a passive attention, a watching, which is earnest in its basis, but not a projecting or creating force. An active attention is one of putting forth effort to achieve an end, which must be decided on beforehand. Since we know nothing directly about realization beforehand, any effort at actively creating it would be just another ego-fantasy. But to listen with attention to what we observe will show us what we are not, leaving us eventually in the position of the silent witness, completely detached from any doing or effort. A relentless listening with attention, not a doing, will lead us into the knowledge of our true state as the unbiased observer. Any effort would be active or creative and therefore not a true inquiry or observation. To be everything, we cannot create the illusion of being any thing. Eventually, even the very act of inquiry will be lost.

To truly surrender to a higher power as a path to realization must also follow this same formula. The idea that surrender means choosing a new, more holy lifestyle is just as mistaken as self-inquiry with a pre-determined image as its goal. Changing one set of values for a new and improved set is not surrender, it is nothing but the ego once again calling the shots. To truly give up one's life is to watch the events of that life unfold before you, remaining as a silent witness, letting God perform the doing. To guide ourselves with effort along a preset path, no matter how holy, virtuous, or "selfless," would be a doing, not a surrender. Here also is needed the simple act of listening with attention. By removing our active attention from what is being done, we remove the sense of the doer, and instead effortlessly watch the mind as it spins its web, whether the web be that of a recluse or householder.

Surrender or inquiry lead to the same still place beyond the mind. Whether we question our very sense of self, or surrender it to a higher power, we are retreating from the individuality-sense, the doer: the creation of the mind. Our sense of what we are is forever changed, losing the sense of separation and angst born of identification with the finite. By watchful inquiry we see the truth; by selfless surrender, we accept it. By ceasing to project and create egos which we then call "I," we leave the game of duality and its never-ending compensation for the calm and quiet of no where and no thing … to die and through death, become aware.

### Poems by Shawn Nevins

The Truth is not hazy.
It is a rock surrounded by mist.
And we are creatures of the mist,
Whose memory is all that gives them form.

All around us dances life.
Yes! Life really is a dance,
Whose sadness at the last note
Is frozen in an eternal now
Resting within oblivion.

Darkness reflects fears,
until you step out
and feel the solidity
that comes from walking through an unfamiliar door
into a familiar room.

Dead, but aware.
Not you, but aware.
Aware of itself,
Awareness without any distinction,
No subject or object.
Eternally unmoving,
Timeless, dimensionless Presence.

It is deadly play and beautiful agony,
This place of perfect dreams.
Where only the dead see motion masquerading as life,
And the eternal, unmoving pulse
Which is utter stillness and our lasting Home
Is seen by the living as little more than a shadow.

Death is turning to face
where you are not,
where you will be,

and where you are.
You've been there all along.
You are not ship's captain.
You are Magnetic North,
the current,
the North Star,
and that deep darkness in which it rides.

Death relieves you of many dreams;
allows you to see that line
between sea and sky
where waves unroll with grace
into open air.
Every step of your life
slips silently from your care,
as these smoky words
trail off into yesterdays.

Winter's wreckage lies strewn about the woods
leaving you to guess the pattern
in this jumble of limbs and leaves.
Last year's aster remains upright, sentinel,
as if saying, "All is well."
All *is* well.

You are not,
Yet you still are,
Only there is not a you.

## Nothing to Be Done? by Bob Cergol

*About the frequent assertion, often expressed convincingly by those who've had partial realizations, that there's nothing to be done, just "be what you already are":*

I think they were not prepared to accept the ramifications and full meaning of what they apprehended, and they've created a bulwark designed to KEEP OUT the "hound of heaven" and keep the self identity intact.

Indeed, I have come to see my own path as one which was fighting off this acceptance. All those years I kept leaving—and returning—to Richard Rose, only to leave again one last time, when I thought I was attempting to move forward on a path; it turns out it was my way of coping with, dodging, evading by any means at my disposal, having to accept what I already knew in my heart to be true but which was too painful to accept—or so I thought. It required Rose "leaving" the scene and a complete stranger whose words caught me off guard when I was all but exhausted from denial. I see this as the story of many, if not all, individual paths. All the while you believe you are fighting your way towards something, it is just your gentle way of comforting yourself as you slowly surrender. In a word, our life is about dying. Every human being is dying a slow death—I mean in precisely the sense we take when we speak of someone gravely ill and dying. We are all desperately learning how to die—coming to terms with it.

Of course how can it be any different. In the ego-centric position, identity spins identity ceaselessly. It never occurs to it that it is not anterior to everything, but itself an object. "I" doesn't have realization any more that it has a soul—or any more than the body has air. It's quite the other way around, air envelopes the body. (Rose wrote, "I am of thee and all that remains of me is thee." He didn't write, "You are in me," or "You are of me.")

These people will have a change of heart when "Death" comes out from the other side of the confessional and they realize they have just confessed their ultimate gambit to their opponent! I say this because they have already seen too much to "take it back."

It is not precise philosophical understanding expressed elo-quently which is solid ground but the acceptance of death which is the basis for true realization. There is a realization and then there is the machine's reaction to it. Partial realization, or the so-called "glimpse," is the refusal to accept the full import of what is seen! This acceptance completely changes the point of reference. You cannot simply "be what your already are." It is "You" who must and will go! You have no choice in the matter.

The "experience of doing nothing" depicts the theme of separate identity believing in death and then denying death. Realization that there is no death because there is nothing to die manifests as an experience by an individuality. It is as though Awareness holds a mirror up and the infinite recursion of reflections is the ceaseless churning of the cosmos. Some infinitesimal particle, itself in fact the whole, "remembers" the mirror. In other words, realization cannot be explained—but in the manifested world of form, there is a reaction to it. That reaction is the experience and varies widely. The common denominator is the awareness of what is and what is not.

"... so you're saying, not only how do I know the garbage you threw over my fence is real, but maybe the <u>fence</u> isn't even real, and ... hey, this is the same trick as last time!"

# 8: Ringing True

## Doing Nothing, All Things Are Done, by Mike Conners

If someone told you the real, true secret to a blissful, contented and stress-free life (life in the state of Self realization)—could you *hear* it? There is a line in the Tao Te Ching, "Abiding in non-doing, nothing remains undone." It sounds good, but it seems to contradict our personal experience and disagrees with almost everything we've heard: "We must *do something* in order to get things done"; "The path to Self realization, and Enlightenment especially, is *long* and *very* difficult"; "Few succeed; perhaps one in a million will begin the path, and of those perhaps one in a million will reach the end!"; "To reach enlightenment you must renounce every thing, even the desire for enlightenment!" We may pay attention to such lines about non-doing, renouncing, and such, which seem paradoxical and very confusing.

Most do not succeed in reaching the goal simply because the goal is a state of Effortlessness. It is abiding in non-doing, and doing cannot lead to non-doing! Effortlessness cannot be had through effort, but we can reach the goal easily and quickly through a daily practice of Effortlessness, and nothing will remain undone.

To realize the truth of this statement, we need to have the *experience* of effortlessness in our daily life. Some find it in sports, some in the arts, and some in desperation. For our purpose, the easiest and most dependable way is thru a practice of Effortlessness in silent meditation. A twice-a-day practice of Effortless meditation gives us the very relaxing, pleasant experience of the automatic nature of thinking and feeling. Soon we become aware of our not being the doer of it. Normally, we say, "I think" and "I feel" or "I am the thinker, the feeler, and the doer" or even "I *am* my thoughts, my feelings, my memories, and my actions." But, with all this illusion of our being the doer, and our identification with thoughts and feelings, comes all our suffering! The practice of Effortless meditation quickly and easily ends this illusion, the identification, and the suffering it brings, by giving us the direct experience of the effortless nature of thinking. This disidentification comes very easily, and quickly, with regular, Effortless practice. It is extremely rare without it. To this end, the most important thought I want to leave with you is this: Along with any other practices you have chosen as your path to Enlightenment,

*Establish a twice-a-day practice of effortless meditation.*

There are many benefits that come automatically from a regular practice:

- ♦ It is easy, pleasant, and deeply relaxing. Deep relaxation brings stress relief, and so benefits our health.
- ♦ Our whole life becomes easier, more pleasant, and finally, completely effortless at all times.
- ♦ Effortless meditation awakens creative levels of the mind, bringing inspiration, intuition and insight.
- ♦ With regular practice of just letting thoughts and feelings come and go, we become less controlling and defensive in our personal relationships, opening us to the experience of unconditional love.
- ♦ For our spiritual purpose, the regular experience of effortlessness leads very quickly to egolessness; the end of our identification with the "I," the imagined thinker, feeler and doer of all actions; Nirvana.

Effortlessness works with all silent meditation techniques: T.M., Zazen, Mindfulness, Prayer of Recollection. Whichever technique we've chosen should be interesting to the mind, and naturally attract our attention.

To meditate effortlessly, we begin by sitting comfortably, with our eyes closed, for half a minute or so. We will naturally begin to feel some relaxation.

Any thoughts, feeling, or sensations we experience will come automatically, effortlessly, and spontaneously. We may become lost in thought for a time ... equally effortlessly....

We will automatically and effortlessly remember that we are sitting there to do our technique. That remembering will be a spontaneous, "Oh! ... I'm sitting to ...." or something like that. As effortlessly as we remember the name of a friend, we will remember our technique.

*At this point it is important that we not try to DO our meditation technique!* A faint remembering of it is enough. It all happens naturally. It is just the way the mind works. We continue to sit, comfortably, just letting it come … and letting it go.

# CYCLE OF
# EFFORTLESS MEDITATION

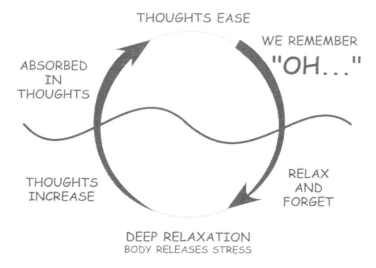

THOUGHTS EASE

WE REMEMBER

"OH..."

ABSORBED
IN
THOUGHTS

THOUGHTS
INCREASE

RELAX
AND
FORGET

DEEP RELAXATION
BODY RELEASES STRESS

At some point we will automatically begin to think or feel something else, or we may again find we've been lost in thoughts. We'll again remember, "Oh! … I'm…." thus effortlessly and spontaneously remembering our technique again. We continue to sit, not trying to meditate, but being aware of whatever is happening. There may be many of these "Oh! …." cycles, or not many. Whatever comes effortlessly is correct Effortless meditation.

In practice we sit like this for 15 or 20 minutes, twice a day:

- No concentration
- No expectations
- No control of thoughts or feelings
- No resistance or clinging to anything
- No effort! It's a natural, automatic process

When we want to end our meditation, we continue to sit for 2 to 3 minutes before opening our eyes.

*Some definitions:*

EFFORT - "The conscious application of mental or physical power" (Webster's Third International Dictionary).
EFFORTLESS - Requiring no effort. Automatic, spontaneous, occurring naturally.
EFFORTLESS MEDITATION - Practice of non-doing; experience of the automatic nature of mind.
EGO - The "I"; the imaginary doer of thinking, feeling, and acting.
NIRVANA - Extinguishing this false "I," bringing us to true Self Inquiry and to Self Realization.

### *Your Treasure House, by Ma Tsu*

*Hui Hai as a young man traveled to the monastery of Ch'an master Ma Tsu about 1,200 years ago and recorded the following conversation:*

Ma Tsu: What do you hope to gain by coming here?
Hui Hai: I have come seeking the Buddha-Dharma (i.e. the Way).

MT: Instead of looking to the treasure house which is your very own, you have left home and gone wandering far away. What for?

HH: Please tell me to what you alluded when you spoke of a treasure house of my own.

MT: That which asked the question is your treasure house. It contains absolutely everything you need and lacks nothing at all. It is there for you to use freely, so why this vain search for something outside yourself?

## Meeting Richard Rose: Notes from 1978, by Art Ticknor

*March 29, 1978*

I had been attending weekly meetings of the Ohio State University "Pyramid Zen" group for the previous five weeks. Richard Rose showed up unexpectedly for the meeting this evening. When I came into the room and saw him, I introduced myself: "You must be Mr. Rose," I said. "My name's Art Ticknor. I know why I'm doing this, and it's for selfish reasons. Why are you doing it?"

In retrospect, I saw that this was rude, but it wasn't my intention. I'd heard that he did all sorts of things and didn't charge for them, so I figured he must have some ulterior motive, and I wanted to get the cards on the table.

He looked at me with a humorous sparkle in his eyes. "First of all, what you're doing isn't selfish. And I do what I do because I can't help it—it's an obsession."

That's all it took to knock the chip off my shoulder. "This guy's okay," I told myself. I sat across from him and started a conversation by asking him about the meaning of his statement (in *The Albigen Papers*) about following the thaumaturgical laws of abstinence to protect yourself from entities.

Rose talked and answered questions during most of the meeting. I felt terrific rapport with him. Most of the things he said rang "true"— i.e., when I heard them verbalized, I recognized them as things I knew nonverbally. For example, you can't force yourself along the path. Some ideas that Rose talked about:

- ♦ You have to set priorities based on what's important to you.

- If you're interested in the spiritual search, it will be fun (not a chore).
- Set a 1-hour meditation period every day. Many, many things will come up to compete with it. It will take about a month to get to the point where you can do some effective introspection toward the end of the hour—and another five months to get in the groove.
- Memories of interaction with parents and siblings are good material for meditation. Realize that you weren't always in the right.
- Anything within the past 2 - 3 years is probably too recent.
- Dreams are a good source of material for meditation. Write them down.
- The biological role or natural purpose of the female is to bear children and be submissive to the male. The role of the male is to protect the female and children.
- When he wrote that you must tell the truth ("Tell the truth in all things relative," in his Threefold Path paper), he did not mean indiscriminately—not to the boss, the cop, the judge, etc.
- Sociologists and psychologists are building a paradigm full of lies. Most psychologists since and including Freud, with the exception of Jung, have been packagers and marketeers.
- All you need to do is listen to the conflicting voices within "yourself."
- Zen is the best method for finding your Self. Give yourself the koan, "Who am I?" There is no real Zen practiced in the US now.
- Committing yourself to helping others on the path will speed up your own search.
- Gurdjieff defined four levels of people (i.e., stages of development): instinctive, emotional, intellectual and philosophical. Only the latter can effectively search for the Truth. Rose said that the first 5 Albigen Papers operate at the intellectual level, hoping to stimulate intuition in intellectual seekers.
- Psychology is extremely simple—only three items: perceiving, recording and reacting.
- Paradox: we don't have free will but we must act as if we did.

♦ Children have great intuition for the first couple years, until we take them from the general to the particular (seduce them, almost). We must learn to be like children again.

There was a margin note in my journal: "He rang bells in me; I felt tremendous joy; afterwards, felt as if I was walking two inches off the ground." I suppose I didn't write more about that because I felt I would never forget the details. What I didn't write:

> At some point in the conversation, a brass gong was struck inside me. I had no idea there even was such a thing. The words that formed in my mind were, "This man is telling the Truth. I've never heard it before, but something in me recognizes it." After the meeting, we adjourned to a McDonald's restaurant in the basement of the student union. Rose continued talking and joking in the same vein as in the classroom upstairs. People at other tables were obviously fascinated by the drift of his remarks that they caught. When I walked out of the McDonald's along the student union corridor, every indication that was coming into my brain said that my feet were honestly not touching the floor. I wasn't hallucinating in terms of thinking that others would see the same thing if they looked at me. But it dawned on me that the phrase "walking on air" wasn't just a loose metaphor and that others had obviously experienced exactly what I was experiencing in sensory perception. The walking-on-air was accompanied by an intense euphoria.
>
> A day or two later, I was scratching my head asking myself what it was that Rose had said that had induced the joy and euphoria that meeting him caused. And it dawned on me what it was: "The answers are all within."
>
> For the previous ten or twelve years I had gone through periodic identity crises (I don't know why I labeled them as such at the time, but in retrospect it was a perceptive label). I had all the things that should have made me happy—wife and kids I adored, career, house, cars—but it wasn't enough. I felt there was some missing meaning or purpose. But I could project every remedy I could think of down the road to acquisition or accomplishment, and they all came up short. I had been scanning the horizon for answers, never stumbling onto the intuitive truth that Rose had verbalized.

*May 11, 1978*

Rose gave a public talk at OSU this evening. I made notes of these items:

- In the final case, there is no mind.
- Rose found no "discrepancy in interlinear meaning" in Paul Brunton's writings. (In other words, he thought that Brunton was honest and without ulterior motive.)
- Each man has to have his own trauma. Let it lead you to ultimate reality.
- Every man has his own path.
- Truth is in the individual—not in a cult or a geographic area.
- Koans are artificial trauma. Like studying mathematics, you can get a *satori* experience. [Satori: momentary "wow!" things fit in place.]
- Changes in the self:
  - o The instinctive level is transcended by a salvation experience, by falling in love with someone or something other than the self.
  - o The resulting emotional level is transcended by a satori or eureka experience.
  - o The subsequent intellectual level is transcended by a cosmic consciousness or unitive experience.
  - o The "fourth way" or philosophical level is transcended by *sahaja nirvikalpa samadhi* or ego death.
- The real answer is inside. Find a system of work. Meditate—wrestle with thoughts—and hope.
- Rose said he learned mind-to-mind transfer through a Zen teacher [long after his own self-realization]. Any true Zen teacher can do this.
- Organizations kill the vital part of you.

х

- *Psychology of the Observer* [an approach to observing the observer that he described in a subsequent book of that title] will bring you to the point [of self-realization] if you stay with it long enough.
- The koan called life will remove your mind for you.

- Rose recommended reading Gurdieff's philosophy through Ouspensky's *Fourth Way*. Rose didn't think that G. or O. had found the ultimate realization, but he thought the material was valuable. Rose said his path, unlike Gurdjieff's, was not a path of extreme observation.

- It's nonsense that you're going to bliss your way to eternity. Trauma is what produces the ultimate experience.

- Man finds God within himself. You have to go through the experience of nothingness.

- It's possible to produce "miracles" without knowing who you are (like a chemist producing reactions).

- Don't continue to lie to yourself. When you see this, quit it. Change your lifestyle, etc., if necessary.

- The only vehicle we have is our mental apparatus. Use it to *become* the Truth. The only way you can do this is by becoming truthful in small things and working your way up.

- The individual self that approaches the Self is the *observer*.

- The somatic mind at work deciding the lifestyle of the vehicle is the *umpire*. You need to get behind the umpire.

и

- When you observe the appetites, the umpire becomes external. The appetites (physical drives) are *not you* because they are observable. [Likewise with the umpire.]

- Then watch your head working—analyze thinking processes. This is the process observer. Wrestle with *gestalts*. Realize that the mind is not you.

- The mind eventually blows up, stops. This results in Oneness.

- You don't overcome egos (pride, morality, etc.) by throwing them away. The egos are taken away when the head explodes.

- There's no such thing as good and evil in this or the next dimension, but man has to be disciplined until he can discipline himself. You need to keep the body neat, build a healthy body and mind so you can take it apart.

- We're a soggy bag which impressions are made on and which makes wild reactions.

- You destroy your path if you eliminate egos in the wrong sequence. Just move away from untruth.
- The umpire is the coordinator of all the voices [egos; desires and fears]. It tries to keep them all alive. It's the watchdog of the somatic department.
- When the observer puts in a factor of spiritual survival, the umpire may encourage it.
- Don't consider letting go of your position in society, keeping yourself looking good, pride, etc.—unless you discover they are lies.

χ

- Release energy for choosing truths.
- If a promotion comes in your job, take it. Don't make a big deal of it.
- Rose said he didn't know why he was born. The blueprint is already made. No point in trying to manipulate it.
- Every person is the end of the ray of the Absolute. Tremendous equality.

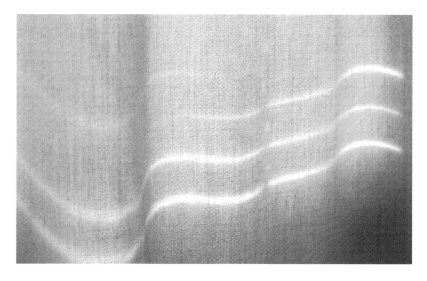

- Intuition is the trip between the emotional and the intellectual approach. It's the only tool you have. Certain things can destroy intuition. An LSD habit, for example. Redevelop the faculty that we're born with. Become as a little child.

- Life is an act, a play. Love is the theme of life. Love is not sex, not hypnosis. Love is friendship and devotion. Love can be hell or happiness.
- You can't work for yourself after you find there's no self. Then work for others. The greatest lovers are the quiet workers for others—for kids, helping people with flat tires, whatever.
- Forget about the lover while you're trying to cultivate the observer.
- Emotional reactions can be good in the search. You only have a few years of your life when your mind is flexible enough to search for truth. Get angry at the phonies [pretending to be teachers] etc.
- Indulge in trauma. You'll find euphoria in the cemetery.

*ж*

- Take a rest at each plateau, then start fighting again.
- You have to fight like hell to find out there's nothing to fight like hell for.
- Allow your concern to stir up your head.
- The process observer watches thinking and feeds info to the umpire. Most of us can't keep a state of mind long enough to solve a problem.
- Words are all foolishness, but we must get on with them until they can be surmounted—direct mind transmission.
- If you dedicate yourself to the Truth, irritations and traumas will arise. Don't hunt trouble and misery. They will come by themselves.
- Mantras are lullabies to keep you from thinking.
- You can't go anywhere unless you help others. Don't wait until you reach an experience. Loan a book, etc. Don't waste it. Keep the laws in mind. [Rose outlines transcendental laws in the 7th chapter of *The Albigen Papers*. The Law of the Ladder states that we shouldn't try to reach down further than the rung below ours.] Wanting to help everyone is ego.
- Rose learned to hypnotize through mind-to-mind contact. He felt that hypnosis is the best way to make people see that man is a robot and that every teacher (psychologist, esotericist) should be a hypnotist, both for demonstration and in order to resist conditioning.

90

♦ The infant and the pure person are safe from possession. Entities [which Rose believed in strongly] are physical creatures which our senses don't pick up. They are not evil per se, but when we break laws, they get in. They're after our energy. They're symbiotic, like pilot fish that guide whales to the feeding ground. Rose believed that everyone has a guiding force—a guardian angel—an intelligence pulling your wires for the good and that everyone is possessed to a degree by both positive and negative entities.

## *Poems by Shawn Nevins*

Do not care for the names of things
or for the particulars.
It is the patterns that call out to you.
For in patterns you find the hand of God —
in names, the hand of man.
All you possess are words.
What you are is a play of light
upon the still hand of eternity.

Don't gather seed for the winter.
There is not enough in this world
or the next.
The way
is to become cold
— a winter landscape —
still, stark, and deep

Yo turn to the world that beats at your door
because this body is tuned to life's needs
and not your soul's.
Where is your true life
among this fog of being?

Where is rest,
satisfaction,
solidity?
Only by remembering the possibilities,
wonder stolen by imagined consequences,
shuddering questions raised by fanciful twilight moments,
and dreams of perfection,
will you close your door to this world,
then, later, let it pass through your empty home.

﹌

Still, ebon pond
like a graveyard at night.
Morning light displays
shimmering motion —
seeming purpose of life.
But the light of darkness doesn't hide,
it reveals,
our essence.

﹌

"Erosion"

Every mouthful is the last,
every opening begins anew.
So say these grey, sprightful little birds
that peep and dash among winter's branches.
Their moment of being
echoes painfully in my ears,
like the Pied Piper
calling away the children.
Each note drowns,
as a stream of silence
undercuts the world.
My friend,
this is neither tragic nor beautiful.

Ethereal fingers of the Absolute
touch the fringes of my mind
like ghosts playing at a harp.
I hear them, but what is really there?
Or did they touch me, but make no sound?
I know people came before me
and walked this very canyon.
They were me,
yet we never were.
Ever deepening silence is the route of my words,
guided by an opening from within,
swallowing all.

God sees the fall of every sparrow.
God is every sparrow.

Every night there are books of poetry
Waiting in the sky.

The sparrow's place is to fall,
God's—to fall and rise again.
Such motion is all that occurs
And is of no consequence.

The books tell stories
All of which, ultimately, are lies.
The sky, with its quiet weight of silence,
Waits between the bones
And the letters which are bones in the making.
I can finish this tale only by stopping.

## *Things to Do, by Shawn Nevins*

1. Fall and rise a thousand times if need be.
2. Become a habitual seeker.
3. Give up, then try again.
4. Realize that you want to help others.

93

5. Be thankful.
6. Become a decent human animal.
7. Look for the source of thoughts.
8. Look in whatever way keeps your attention.
9. Will to do one thing—one iron in the fire.
10. Find a teacher(s).
11. Always desire more, never be content.
12. Surround yourself with fellow seekers.
13. Spend time alone.
14. Know that the Hound of Heaven is real.

1. *Fall and rise a thousand times if need be:* I know some people who will set a goal to meditate every morning, do so for a week, then give up after they miss a morning. They despair over their temporary failure. The key is to keep at it, even if you miss every other day. Even if you never manage to meditate every single morning, to keep trying is what matters. If you approach the task in that manner, you will discover of what you are capable, and what you are—likely different than your original conception.

2. *Become a habitual seeker:* The same idea as Richard Rose's vector. With enough time, you become someone who continually questions the world around and inside of them. You will want to know the truth of matters and be open to more than one possibility or the easy answer. Your eyes and ears will always be open to new sources of information.

3. *Give up, then try again:* You can't control this one, but it is useful to know that it will occur. There is some magic in the process of giving up, as it weakens our conception of what we are. Our conceptions of our self as a seeker are stripped away, leaving only Rose's "egoless vector" which searches simply because there is nothing else to do. This temporary giving up is also the rest period necessary for any exercise.

4. *Realize that you want to help others:* The ego prevents us from reaching out to others. With persistent self-analysis, you will come to have true consideration for your fellow man—you will see your flaws in others and others' flaws in you. There is the thought that we should help others because it will help us in the long run, but this is not the same as truly wanting to help another. It is a milestone when we want to help simply because it is the natural reaction.

5. *Be thankful:* You are fortunate to be willing and able to ask questions of self-definition. You are fortunate for this day of possibilities stretching out in front of you. There is a bit of magic in giving thanks, as doing so recognizes that we are not the center of the Universe and relinquishes some of our imaginary control of life.

6. *Become a decent human animal:* Meaning that with honest introspection, you will become more compassionate and less defensive as you recognize your vanities. Also entails learning how to provide for yourself in the world. On a physical and social level, we become more at ease and better players of the game. You do not need to become a saint or an expert mechanic, however.

7. *Look for the source of thoughts:* Or look for the source of feeling, or intuition. Whatever you believe yourself to be, look to find where it originates. This will lead you to the source of your self. This question is phrased in many ways and may change over time. I began wanting to know what my purpose was, and ended by wanting to know what (if anything) was unchanging within me. Richard Rose describes this as backing away from untruth, which is correct in that we should not postulate what we might find. However, there is an intuition of the eternal within us which is helpful to follow—a garbled message from the Absolute.

8. *Look in whatever way keeps your attention:* You will get bored of looking within. Keep looking for teachers and methods, so that when you come to the end of your current way, you won't lose time wandering in search of another. Every person must find their own way—a customized method of going within. You must craft your own key.

9. *Will to do one thing—keep one iron in the fire:* Focus is the solution to any problem. If you are trying to play the stock market, get a promotion, find a spouse, and get a college degree, you will obviously have trouble finding time to meditate, read, and seek out spiritual teachers. Time spent looking within is rewarded with proportional results—up to a point. Like any exercise, rest is part of the equation.

10. *Find a teacher(s):* A teacher is a friend with more experience on the spiritual path. It may be a series of teachers—each giving you a tool to use in your inner exploration. A book or tape may be as important as a living person.

11. *Always desire more, never be content:* There are side benefits to a spiritual search. One may make fascinating friends, have travel opportunities, may even be regarded as a teacher in their own right, all before finding an answer to their deepest question. There arises the temptation to settle for a lesser prize. This is a powerful temptation whose only cure is to project out your life strand and ask if you are heading where you want to be. When you are old, what will you want to say about your life? When it is just you facing the unknown, where will you find certainty?

12. *Surround yourself with fellow seekers:* There is tremendous benefit to associating with like-minded people. Better yet, is sharing an apartment or house with a group of seekers. It is a resource of ideas and inspiration, as well as help with the everyday problems of life. You will learn from each other's successes and failures. When one member is in despair, his fellows can in a sense, carry him until he recovers. If the group is too small, less than four perhaps, then the odds are the number of depressed members will outweigh the number of inspired and drag down the whole lot.

    Because each spiritual path is unique, it is difficult to work with a group. Groups tend to either homogenize or break apart. However, if the majority of members are sincerely seeking (looking within), this will enable diversity and understanding.

13. *Spend time alone:* From a few minutes a day to weeks-long isolations. This is a time to evaluate what you have accomplished and where you want to go. It is a time of intense concentration, intense looking within. When alone, it is easier to realize that we are the sole judge of our life and what matters is that we find the thing which settles our soul. A person may camp out, get a cheap motel room, go to a retreat center, or even hide out in their own room.

14. *Know that the Hound of Heaven is real:* Refers to the poem by Francis Thompson. There is something calling you—God, Rose's Invisible Current, or the Voice of the Silence. Become aware of your intuition (heart), your hunger and yearning for certainty. You hide with endless diversions from your hunger and yearning. You fill the emptiness in you with material goods, or even love. Yet, you are truly, always alone. There is simply you and a haunting question that sooner or later you must confront.

# 9: The Penny That Blots Out the Sun

### The Penny That Blots Out the Sun, by Alfred Pulyan

It was in the little western town of Berree. I faced the committee. Mr. Aleph Norte, the chairman, looked at me severely. "You know our principles," he said. "Seek and ye shall seek. Knock and we hope nothing happens."

"I do," I replied. I knew that Mr. Norte had had a very trying month. On his arrival at Berree, he had made no secret that he was and always had been a gold-seeker. There was an avalanche. Many sought to sell him their mines; many, however, offered them to him freely. It was necessary to impose stringent conditions. The gold must be officially assayed at 100 percent, it must be on the surface, it must be near at hand. Even then a committee was necessary to strain out all the applicants.

"I notice in your offer," said Mr. Norte, "that the gold is pure and beautiful and lies on the surface ready for the taking. However, you state that it lies on a road half-a-mile to the north. Now, all of us here know for a certainty that there cannot be only one way. We are here to investigate every way and are willing to spend our money and time in continual seeking. We are, therefore, sorry to refuse your offer, the more so as we love people."

This was not the first time I had made a mistake. Without thinking, I blurted out the truth. *"Actually, the gold lies in a half-mile circle. It is all around you. You cannot fail to find it—if, of course, you wish."*

There was a tense and terrible silence. Then, they came towards me.

How did I escape? I did not. The place was a shambles. There were bits of me all over the place, and so I feel free to tell you what the committee would not listen to—the actual way in which a student is brought to "awakening," always has been and, as you will easily see for yourself, always will be—until our species develops a new faculty or somebody bursts this ball.

Your first problem is a teacher, "opener," master, or whatever you like to call him (or her). Let us take a specific example: Subud. This rests on perfectly valid experiences of Muhammad Subuh of Java; in particular on one that happened on the night of June 21-22, 1933.

As has happened many times in history (with the "Buddha" Gautama as an example), a "movement" started from this one man and has become world-wide. Groups of people are meeting everywhere under the guidance of so-called "helpers," and from these, people who are suitable will proceed to centers for direct work.

Awakened and "matured" persons will be needed to do this work. All must derive from Pak (Father) Subuh himself. Awakening may take anything from 30 minutes to 10 years or more, and usually takes several years under favorable conditions. Further, this awakening varies and many do not have either the desire or capacity to awaken others, and rest content with their attainment, spreading what light they can to those around them.

Groups are everywhere in the world. What will happen to this flood of people? Clearly, Subud will develop into a sort of religion and will offer much consolation to those content with the meetings and unable or unwilling to proceed further. That is, in fact, what religions are. There are tens of thousands of awakened people in the U.S., but if these "work," they work alone, and converts to Subud, who trust Pak Subuh, do not trust them.

On the other hand, there is a Zen Master in this country (or soon should be) and those working with him would not be much inclined to switch to Subud.

It seems that there are as many brands of awakening as of coffee, and that it is the well-advertised ones that attract people. They do not differ much actually in method and not at all in result since, as you will see, their problem is the same.

How can we sum this up? Clearly, Zen is a sure way because a succession of enlightened Masters is rigidly maintained, but it is apt to be a very lengthy process. It is also a tough one, but so it has to be in any system. Even in Subud there is an "O" group kept separate because of their violent reactions.

Many are afraid of the whole business because they suspect or rationalize that it is autosuggestion. I know very well, for what it is worth to you, that you are more free than before, not less free. Moreover, if it is time for you to start this process, you will not have much to say about it anyway. We have a saying that when the student is ready the master appears. It does seem to work that way.

The harvest, however, is plentiful but the laborers are few.

Let me consider the problem of working with a person like you, the reader. Normally, if you wish to know something you get a book on the subject or attend lectures or ask a friend. If the subject is not too complicated, you anticipate that, by directing your mind and memory to it, you will see "what it is all about" and finish up with a good working knowledge of the subject. If the subject is very important, your mind becomes as alert as a tiger. It is the way of our minds (and many of the new calculating machines) to dichotomize, to tear things in half. Unfortunately, this process does not work with any "ultimate" problem and only results in the mind breeding more and more thoughts about it unendingly—like grasshoppers.

It so happens that the peculiar origin of you and the universe is concealed in a place that the mind cannot reach. Some persons will call this "God," but this word will mislead you and it is better to find out what this is yourself and then call it what you like.

Most persons think of themselves as twofold. There is "my" consciousness, "my" mind, "my" self on the one hand—and on the other, "my" body. This is all of me. There is a decided split between these two sides of me.

However, the fact is all of these are one; that is, my mind and my body are one—one organism, not two.

But this does not exhaust the situation. There is a pure Consciousness—Consciousness that knows itself. "I am that I am." This is unexpected and I did not believe when I first heard this that there could be two kinds of Consciousness. I only knew the one I was naturally familiar with, the "I am as I am."

The way it works is this. This pure Consciousness shines on the mind-and-body organism; it is the "light that lighteth every man that cometh into this world." When it does this it suffers a change. My mind accepts it only as "my consciousness"—a limited consciousness—and, since Its essence is Self-Consciousness, "I" experience It in a similar way as a self, in fact "myself," or ego. I say I am "conscious of myself," but this is a smaller self, not the Universal One, merely what I call "me," one of my many "me's."

It may be said that the pure Consciousness is concealed in "my" consciousness as a penny may hide the sun. A ray of this may suddenly dazzle us in so-called "mystical experiences," of which most persons have had a touch, but in awakening (or satori or metanoia) we see the pure Consciousness shining serenely in its own light. It is a triumphant experience since "what has to be done" has been done, but it is also profoundly humbling as our little self sees itself as a usurper, a thief borrowing its selfhood from the Universal Self.

A student wrote me: "Consciousness sees itself. It is impossible yet it happens."

So much for theory. The practical job of awakening someone consists in part of showing him or her by various devices that all mental attempts to reach the pure Consciousness are in vain. It lies back of our mind and back of our consciousness. Any thought we have about it is impartially irradiated by it. For example, we think "this is unproved idiocy" and the pure Consciousness lights it up in its usual benevolent way so that it becomes "I am aware that I think this is unproved idiocy."

Obviously, this is a peculiar situation. This Consciousness is at all times ready to make us "aware" of what we are thinking or perceiving, but that does not mean that we become aware of That which is Itself giving us this peculiar faculty of being aware of ourselves and our processes. Thus we get no clue as to whether our thought was a correct one or not; only that we know we have such a thought.

No wonder It is hidden and confusing. The problem is to reach Consciousness as it is in itself and not as reflecting some thought or perception of ours that is in it at the time.

We require empty Consciousness so to say. Some try, like the Yogis or some of them, to attain it by emptying the mind by "meditation" but it is not the mind we have to empty. The real obstacle, of course, is the "my" concept, the self or ego. This is my Enemy in this work. How can we get from "my" consciousness to "the" Consciousness?

Naturally, as long as "we" decide or "we" try to do this, we are regarding ourselves as ultimate and reinforcing the bonds of delusion. All we do is rotate our own ideas like a squirrel in a cage. It would seem, therefore, an impossible task like lifting ourselves up by our own bootstraps.

However, the simple fact is that it happens all the time. There is help from the side of the Consciousness itself (theologians call this "Grace") which is not resting idly but presses to "come out" in us. There are intimations of what this pure Consciousness is like in music and the arts, in nature, and the highest aspirations we have.

The teacher (I wish I had a better word) takes advantage of these. Further, he stays "open" with the student, and the student, by mere love and friendship, receives what in Zen is called "transmission" and in Subud "contact." It is inevitable that the student should carefully observe every word and action of the teacher (because at first he doubts him) and in time the awakening of the teacher is felt definitely by the student, although not verbally definable.

In Zen, so-called "koans" are used to throw the mind out of the reasoning rut (in these days of paper books, I assume the reader knows what koans are) and sudden shocks are contrived to shake out the obstinate ego. The teacher uses similar things.

For months, the student tries every possible argument. Over and over, he will bring up, for example, the "problem of evil," the question of life after death, of reincarnation, of some religion or other he may have been taught in childhood, of science, of his own desperation at ever getting anywhere, of how one can tell if the realization, if it comes, is any more "real" than anything else, if it is merely another trick of the versatile mind or subconscious, whether we are just bubbles—anything and everything.

It is nothing new to the teacher. He could write the script himself. (In fact, I have partly done so here.) However, he remains steady; he knows what has to be done, he knows where the student is and in time he sees hopeful signs.

The student is disturbed. He has come to the end of his "tricks" (actually desperate attempts to preserve the ego as boss, when it is only a competent executive officer) and the teacher will not "buy" any of such tricks.

The student is not a fool. He knows all the time what he is doing and that one day he must surrender in utter helplessness. Meanwhile, he retains a second line of defense, a "secondary" judgment which does not yield whatever he may say openly. One day this too lapses, even if only for a moment.

Then something happens. The student is surprised to notice, for example, that his perceptions are sharper, everything seems brighter. Next morning he awakens to a situation which puzzles him for a moment. Something is missing. What can it be?

He soon finds out. For a time he enjoys the extraordinary experience of being a limited ego with an unlimited Consciousness. He is free to use it and to test it. He finds It will show him the basis behind material things, the many in the One, a clear but absolutely new and indescribable thing; or it makes clear once and for all, the whole process of the ego or self in himself and others and in relationship. For a salesman or lawyer, this is indeed a bonanza, but there is a price to pay—he is not likely to use this new wisdom for wrong.

He now knows intimately—more intimately than we can know anything or anybody—the Basis of our universe and us and is perforce henceforward a "channel" and a servant of "That." It is a strange feeling for a proud man.

The job is not done. There ensues a long maturing process. Confused areas of thought, mental blockages, must yield one by one. He has the means to do this, but uses it naturally. One day the last weed is gone from his garden and he is surprised to find he has no further questions.

Do not think that this is all a mental exercise. It involves the whole organism, body and mind. It is a criticism of Zen that this feature is not stressed at all. In Subud, remarkable cures have occurred and readers may remember another great man who went about doing good—he could not avoid it. People will not flock for enlightenment, but will try anything to cure a so-called chronic condition.

What happens to the student after his experience has matured? It becomes the most natural thing in the world. He may say, like Gautama, that he has done nothing at all. It is true that he has "done" nothing, but he does know by actual experience what our human situation really is.

There is much difference between experience and words. You are welcome to laugh at my words. I do not think you would laugh at the experience.

Do not find this article too disturbing. You will find that God is both "open" and loving—devastatingly, almost unbearably, so.

If you should find that the thought of God is constantly in your mind, do not try to remove it; it can be very unsettling. Welcome it and in time it will seem supremely right.

Always treat children like adults and adults like children, and you'll never go wrong. ~ *Musician/author Kinky Friedman's father*

If A equals success, then the formula is A equals X plus Y plus Z, where X is work, Y is play, and Z is keep your mouth shut. ~ *Attributed to Albert Einstein*

From there to here, and here to there, funny things are everywhere. ~ *Dr. Seuss*

Frisbeetarianism (n), the belief that, when you die, your soul goes up on the roof and gets stuck there. ~ *Author unknown*

*Questioner:* What do you think about modern civilization?
*Mohandas Gandhi:* I think it would be a good idea.

# 10: Becoming the Truth

## *You Can Only Become the Truth, by Gary Harmon*

You can't know the truth, but you can become the truth. You are what you do, not what you know. Spiritual change is a process which will change the state of mind and result in a change in the state of being.

There are several things we can do to center ourselves so that we can think more clearly. There are more than a few writings that advise to become as a little child. That early state that we all have witnessed was innocent and carefree for the most part. Before the age of two and a half we don't really consider ourselves as a separate, singular individual—we are better defined as the entire world from that perspective. Then we are told that we are that one in the mirror and start believing we are that reflection. At a latter age, especially after puberty, that freedom of early childhood is seldom realized again for we grow up to become adults with adult problems.

Consider what a period of chastity might reveal. To again center the mind and live as a child aware of awareness, not adult and social style games—is this possible? Yes, it can rationally be done. As an experiment you might try purposely abstaining for twenty-eight days and take a vacation from the normal routine. Of course, if married this may require special considerations. Sound radical? OK, but we have a unique mission if we care to take the challenge of absolute self-discovery. The peace that most attempt to find is only relative peace. Relative peace comes and goes, but what if it were possible to attain a more stable tranquility? Chastity is a way of shutting the doors to outside influences that are like waves that rise and fall. There is no better way to develop the intuition and become less of an animal and more in tune with your true being.

Psychological—for lack of a better word—enquiry is truly essential for assisting and gauging our progress as we go thru different phases that will result in a permanent change of being.

Realization is about understanding, not about making your life work or accumulating wealth, fame and security. It is not something added to your existing circumstance, or a sense of existence you are trying to improve upon. It is more of a simplifying and coming to terms with your life. It is a backing away from wrong conclusions which have become delusions and hinder a direct view of what *is*. The search is a subtraction process that results in the only apparent life which is left after removal of the exposed shadows. One should utilize whatever is necessary in the field of psychosomatic tools and utilize common sense to better see how we fool and patronize ourselves.

The result is a different perspective from the herd mentality that relishes its animal programming as being who one really is. Our society has accepted silicone gel packs, anorexia, plastic surgery and blood rerouting as a reality which somehow makes us better and more exceptional human animals.

You are what you do, not what you know, and you can not learn the truth, you can only become it. So with that in mind determination is not enough; it requires action. In other words, you have to get beyond the physical so that you can clearly see yourself and what you are doing. It's like finding out that you have been kicking yourself without realizing it, causing your own pain. That's all your fantasy of a separate identity amounts to. However, as long as you're trying to make the fairy-tale work out one way or another, you can't really observe yourself because you are the agonizing activity you're trying to observe.

There is only awareness. You do not really even exist—not as it seems, at any rate.

To cross over and then return will require all the energy we can muster and usually requires a lifetime of effort. It must be an all or nothing intention, which is why it is best to begin this course at an early age. Even death can not be dreaded. You must take the fear of death and turn that into the death of fear. That is when factual self-observation begins and not before.

To retreat from error and not tolerate untruth on any level is to live the path of the determined spiritual seeker. A quitter never wins and a winner never quits. It takes one-pointedness of direction to transcend the bondage of clinging to a sham identity. Liberation is living a profound understanding of this principle.

## Poems by Shawn Nevins

Once again I travel down through the years.
What is this eye that never sleeps?
What is this fact that tears my mind?
Ages of living, working, dying,
like wheat swaying in the breeze.
These lovely, painful cycles of existence,
falling and rising.
In my heart is the solidity of the pivot point
rooted in a foundation of nothingness.
Nothing is more impenetrable —
nothing more solid, than nothing.
I drift between life and love —
between vision and the eye itself.

❧

God does not enter empty rooms.
He is the empty room.
All that stands in his way
Is a silly fellow trying to empty the room.

❧

### "Face of God"

Nothingness looks out
And Nothingness looks in.
My eyes are hollow;
Space pervades all.
A wind blows quietly through empty halls.

❧

He came to us as a man selling air
And we all thought twice at the offer and price
Of this thing which seemed so rare.
Was he dreaming, or really There?

Of his formula I only know
Bits and pieces of what he told:

Live the Truth, be not shy, unlock your heart,
Fear not to die, help your friend along the Way,
From untruth back away.

His map is there, the last mile up to you.
Die to live—the paradox is true.
Full of anguish over here, full of joy over there,
You were never, never anywhere.

"Home"

I am waiting for you
at the edge,
where thought is held by riveted attention,
and self begins to slip away.
I am there,
where you and I become welcoming waters —
pure, dark, deep, and full.
Where all is lost
and all is found
in this ever deep, ever still home.

I look through the years
like a man peering down
a dark tunnel.
The light of my life
illuminating such a short way.
The noise of water that pours forth
and bars my way from whence I came,
is the same for every man.
It is that eternal motion
from the Source.
We are but leaves in the water
settling to the bottom as we are
worn to shreds.
Peering down the tunnel,
we peer into our nature,
and the light of all life
is enough to illumine the Truth.

"Frank Hurley"

A dying man stays awake
all night
and won't lie down.
Not because he is afraid,
but because he wants to See.
Like a dream waits for day,
all his life he's waited
for this night.
Finally,
he doesn't have to be
anything,
anymore.

## *Nothing of You Will Remain, by Bob Cergol*

*The following was in response to a writer's comment about feeling disconnected, de-motivated, and so forth:*

I know this much: it's all based on a LIE. If you looked at that mood as a whole and perhaps in your case—I'm just going on what was typical for me—saw that the mood was the result of your realization or thoughts—right or wrong, that all your ideas about searching have been for naught, a complete waste—and that all that you've thought you've been doing is also for naught—a complete waste, a game to pass the time because you have nothing better to do—well understandably this sort of inkling is not inspirational—it is deflating. But it is only deflating because you still have a desire to get the answer, to become better than you, etc. More precisely, you still believe that you could cheat death somehow. impossible. Nothing of you will survive. If you could admit that you've been kidding yourself—the ultimate form of self-honesty—that you will live and die in ignorance—because there is no hope for you— just where would that leave you? What would you do then?

The truth is that you, and everyone else, never will have an experience. Who you really are is not an experience. The self you identify with is the "experience." Your real Self observes it. Your real Self just IS—is all there is. So as Pulyan said, after death "Nothing of you remains."

Perhaps all that's needed is one more small step to letting go.

As I see it, the ego is a fiction, a lie, a contraption—born of the body—and the experience of self-consciousness is only made possible by that which animates all form. (The light shining through the pumpkin animates the pumpkin, so the pumpkin speaks: "I think, therefore I am.")

The ego cannot accept the truth because it is based on the body's wiring, which wants to survive—in spite of the obvious future evidence to the contrary. The ego secures itself like an oyster with layer upon layer of constructs—it's automatic and inexorable.

Analyzing the constructs is useful—but is literally just scratching the surface. This sort of activity easily, naturally, automatically becomes outward focused. It becomes a device used by ego to maintain ego. (Ego 1 looking at ego 2.) It is not looking at the looker—except for maybe an instant—when there is a momentary newness to the effort and amounts to asking: "Who am I?" We constantly need new shocks to literally be startled by the question or observation; otherwise the "Who am I?" becomes a meaningless mantra, or mental noise.

Rose said, "It is the task of the seeker of eternity to die while living."

Pulyan said, "You must quit the egocentric position."

I think we underestimate our belief in the body. We think we understand that we are not the body and associate with the mind. You are aware of identity. From where does that identity spring? A long, long time ago, experiences began happening to a body (that had a light shining through it). Those experiences created identity. Memories were recorded. Memories reinforced and built identity. There is a long history to that identity you know and love so well and take as you.

Well, you should know that the body dies and is dissipated. Know, too, that the mind, which is at all times one with that body, likewise is dissipated. nothing of you will remain.

Can you accept that? Right now?

## The Mind in Time, by Bob Fergeson

We've drifted down a line to time
upon a Ray from That which shines.
It shines within in Now, not then,
in Now we live, not "if only when."
We've fallen down to mind in time.

We fell to mind that lives in time
bound to things that live and die.
We tie the knots in our true life-line
and lose the path to That which shines.
Ignorance ties these knots in time
that bind us into finite mind.

What sword, what axe could cut this knot
that Gordon tied to bind our lot?
A little here, a little there,
will never undo this wicked snare.
To cut the knot, this tie that binds,
will take a blade from beyond the mind.

Climb up the line back out of time
To leave our self, our proud dead mind,
To leave the things that thinking brings
For the One Clear Note of Presence's Ring.

Take faith and help from those that find
men are more than plugged-up knots in time.
Silence true gives us a clue
To leave the "I," the "me," the "you."

Take hope, and leave the mind in time,
To listen again to That which shines.

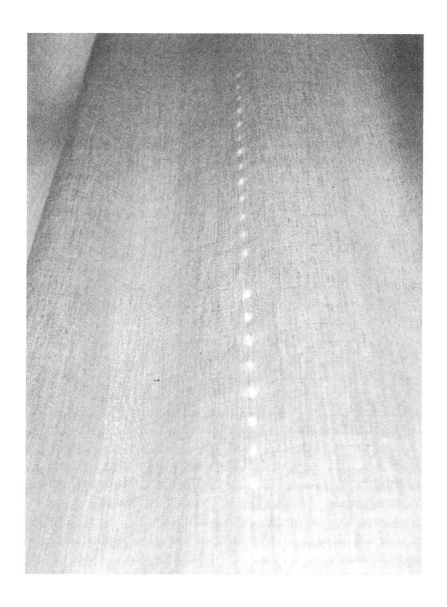

# 11: STALKING YOURSELF

## *Strategies, by Bart Marshall*

As I turned over all those rocks on my spiritual search, I was always trying out recommendations about what I could do to hurry this process along—what I could do, what I could be, to speed things up. Even if the teaching was that there is nothing to be done, I'd want to know what the technique was for *not-doing*. Always thinking it was up to me whether or not this was going to happen.

But is it up to me? Can this shift in perception be brought about by the efforts of an illusory individual? Some teachers say there is absolutely nothing a person can do to bring about this experience, so don't bother. Even teachers like Rose who recommend extreme effort on the spiritual path say that those efforts are not what bring about the experience, if indeed one happens. As Rose says, "There's no recipe for a lightning bolt."

Statistically, though, people who report having a conclusive spiritual experience are usually those who've spent considerable time pursuing spiritual activities. So of course, like everything else on the "path," it's a paradox.

The spiritual path, if we are going to call it that, seems to be a process of maneuvering the mind onto shaky ground, into a state of uncertainty that makes it vulnerable to intervention by an "outside" force. A very delicate contortion. The question is not really "How can I bring about a spiritual experience?" but "How can I become susceptible to Grace? How can I become accident prone?"

From that angle, it seems these general practices are the kind of things that might help maneuver the mind into a vulnerable state. Nothing new here. These ideas are scattered all throughout the teachings and literature. And of course some are in apparent contradiction with each other. In no particular order:

### Absorb Teachings

Do the research. Study what's been said and done before. Turn over every rock, as Rose said, but doubt everything. Let it soak in but don't believe a word of it. Neither believe nor disbelieve. Neither accept nor reject. Just let it all rattle around in there.

### Assume Authority

Work out your own salvation. Take responsibility. Be your own disciple. Trust your innermost experience. People give over responsibility for their health to doctors, and for their salvation to priests and gurus. It makes no sense. Harding: "You are the sole and final authority on what it's like being you. On what is happening right where you are." Buddha: "Be a lamp unto yourself. Be a refuge to yourself. Look not for refuge in anyone beside yourself."

### Focus Intent

Purify, focus and refine intent. Is Truth what you really want? For most so-called seekers, self-realization is not really their greatest desire—it is a means to an end. We want to be self-realized because we think it will improve our lives in some way—bring peace of mind, power, approbation. Also, we're too scattered, full of conflicting desires. Beware of conscious and sub-conscious desires sabotaging spiritual aspirations.

### Cease Knowing

Possibly the single biggest obstacle to realization is thinking you already know what's going on. Stop thinking you know anything. Return to the child-like state of wonder, unknowing, mystery. Have only questions, never answers. If an answer comes, question it. Return to unknowing. Only an empty cup can be filled. Become a vacuum of unknowing and God will rush in.

We think we already know 95% of the truth ("I'm a substantive being with my own consciousness in an infinitely vast, infinitely old universe of separate, real objects ....") and just need answers about that last 5%. We don't want to entertain the idea that the 95% we're standing on is 100% wrong.

Rose was always asking people, "What do you know for sure?" Always trying to prod them into questioning their beliefs. Knowing is Original Sin—in the sense of the true meaning of the word *sin*, which is "to err, to miss the mark." Christianity implies it's knowledge of sex that kicks mankind out of paradise. No. It's any and all knowledge. If any knowing whatsoever is present, you are on the wrong side of the gates. You have drifted into illusion. Knowledge is ignorance. God is unknowing.

### Investigate Personhood (What am I?)

This is the classic path of self-inquiry. Who am I? What am I? Not an analysis of personality traits, but real inquiry into the true nature of self. Is there a self? Is there a person named "I"? Nisargadatta: "You think you are a person who was born, has parents and memories, and will someday die. You are not." When I first read that I got chills. I was never again safe from that thought. The only way out was through it.

What is the mechanism of memory? We rely heavily on memory for our sense of self, for our personhood. But what is memory? In *Blade Runner*, the replicant babe Harrison Ford falls for argues that she is real because she has memories. She tells about seeing a spider when she was 4-years old or something. But her memories are just implants, part of her programming. She's a robot, fresh off the assembly line, programmed with a lifetime of memories. How is that different from your experience of memory?

116

**Practice Inlooking (Where am I?)**

Look directly at the source of looking. Where is the receiver, the processor of the experience now on display? Ask without answering. Ask without knowing or "almost" knowing. Ask without holding onto a base paradigm into which revelation must fit. When you look without knowing, what do you find at ground zero? Where exactly is ground zero? At the exact GPS coordinates of the most intimate pinpoint of your awareness, is anyone home?

Harding experiments like the one we did earlier [that day of the TAT 2005 Spring Conference] are a prime example of this kind of inquiry. There are many other techniques for this and you can make up your own. This type of self-inquiry seeks to answer the question "Where am I?" and uses vision and attention more than thought. The basic idea is to relocate your attention from external objects to the source of looking—to look at the looker.

I used to do this by trying to turn my physical vision around 180 degrees—to stand in front of myself and look back through my own "face." I just couldn't make it work using that image. Too many mental contortions.

For me what works better is to keep the same visual position—looking out—but simply reel attention back in until it rests at ground zero of my experience, at the exact GPS coordinates of the source of my view. Attention is not the same as vision, though they are closely aligned when the eyes are open. Separate them. Bring attention back towards you like a target at a pistol range until it comes to rest at the source of looking.

You can do this anytime, anywhere. Look out as usual. I see people, walls, books. My attention is naturally and habitually drawn to objects "out there." Now let attention come towards you until it rests in the middle distance—in the empty space between the source of looking and the nearest object in front of it. Now let attention rest in as close as it gets—ground zero, zero inches—at the source of all that is arrayed before you. What do you find there?

**Apprehend Time (When am I?)**

Investigate time in the same way you investigate personhood. Chip away at the concept of time like you chip away at the sense of identity. Step out of the apparent flow of time and take a look at it. Can you catch time in the act? Can you experience duration? Is a skeleton or photograph in the present proof of a past? Where is past and future? Where is now? Where is the exact point that future becomes present and present becomes past? What does that pinpoint of presence feel like? Can you feel past and future?

## Abandon Hope

The opening line of a sutra by the third Zen Patriarch of China reads: "The Great Way is not difficult for those who have no preferences." Rose called this "betweenness." It's a way of holding your head as you go about the business of life. Do, but don't care. Do without expecting results. It is a kind of surrender. Do whatever you do without expecting good things to come of it.

## Favor Simplicity

Mental and physical circumstances have an effect on the amount of time and energy available for the search, so it's an advantage to maintain a clean, well-ordered life. As Rose used to say, get your house in order. Limit complexities. Tie up loose ends. Arrange your life for clear thinking.

Also, favor intellectual simplicity. Occam's Razor: the simplest answer is usually correct. Watch how your mind loves complexity. Complexity is in the opposite direction of Truth.

## Choose Silence

Silence is the medium of transmission. Silence inside and out. You can't hear if you're not listening. When silence is an option, choose it. Turn off the car stereo. Turn off TV. Stare into space with no agenda. Listen. Cultivate no-thought.

## Befriend Death

Zen is sometimes described as "learning how to die." People reporting a spiritual realization agree that the person they thought they were was not present for the experience. For myself, I can say there was no trace of Bart whatsoever, not a shred, not a thought—so gone he never was, and no one to care to look for him. The mind has no way of labeling this except to say "death."

Befriend death. An unprepared and overly-fearful mind may fight realization because it seems like death, so it's often recommended we come to grips with our own physical death as part of our spiritual preparation. Get comfortable with the messy ways bodies die. Meditate on your own death. Read *How We Die.* Volunteer with Hospice. Anything that might help dilute the fear of death.

## The Other Side, by Bob Cergol

What sound was it that you first heard
That made those ears your ears to hear?
*And in such hearing spawned the fear*
*Of the other side—the silence here.*

What sight was it that you first saw
That made those eyes your eyes to see?
*And in such seeing spawned the vision:*
*An "I" in loneliness imprisoned.*

What movement made first filled your breath
And made that breath your own to breathe?
*And in such moving brought the gasp*
*That one such breath will be your last.*

What shape was made with flesh and bone
That made this form your form alone?
*A mortal form where thoughts resolved*
*That "I" as form will be dissolved.*

What story told first touched your heart
And made its theme "a thing apart"?
*That heartfelt telling does portend*
*Where flowed life's rhythms—all will end.*

What words were they that left those lips
Through which the Source became eclipsed?
*In darkness, separate shadows grew*
*As animated forms, with speech imbued.*

What choice occurred that made that choice
The one to which you lent your voice?
*And in that lending broke apart*
*From That—the center of your heart.*

What thing is this that strives to BE
An individuality?

119

*—It's just an echo of the other side*
*In which all things here do abide.*

From the other side your being came;
On this side came identity.
From the other side there comes the call
"Your self is here, not there at all."

On the other side of "I am this"
Is "I am not," and "I am nothing."
But in that nothing is your Being
And in that Being—everything.

*Author's note: The original inspiration or idea behind it was from a meeting here a few weeks ago, when D_ was talking about the "I Am" or "Who Am I" meditation/mantra he was doing, and I made some remark about there being "something on the other side of 'I Am'" that his doing of the meditation/mantra was not revealing because that point of reference was contradictory to the point of reference for the meditation. The contradiction was that his meditational point of reference, at least in part, was one of serving the personal identity, which always wants to build on identity. The perspective of the "other side" is ruled out in advance by this personal viewpoint since it would amount to a total acceptance of the personal self's mortality. The idea was to paint a picture*

*of how the "I" arises out of experience and loses its connection with the Source and then re-finds itself. When and how did your sense of "I" first appear?*

*What was the first sound that awakened "I" in you and closed your ear to the Silent Source? What sight first cemented you in this vision of reality that blinded you to the True Light?*

## *Stalking Yourself with the Listening Attention*
### *by Bob Fergeson*

Above the door to the ancient temple in Delphi were inscribed the words, "Know Thyself." These words describe the process by which we separate from our false state of ignorance and rediscover true Being. But how do we initiate this process, this grand work of spiritual discovery? What tools should we choose to come to know this thing we call "ourselves"? If we are to engage in the pursuit of self-definition we will need to use the best tools available. To stalk our "self," we will need something above or behind this personality to best observe with, something of a different order. Using the personality to observe the personality simply doesn't work. It's like trying to lift a plank while standing on it. This self we wish to come to know is a constantly changing, moving target, a veritable chain of reactions and patterns, seldom still, but always within our sight. To observe it we will need something calm and constant. Something that looks but doesn't react; a seeing that listens.

Spending time alone, in a quiet environment, can be a good way to start this practice of self-observation. To be free of the routines of work and family and the expectations of society is calming and conducive to beginning the art of introspection. We can let our guard down a bit. Also, our own personality is partially absent. The part of us that interfaces with others is no longer needed, and we can relax. This state of lack of attack can be quite useful for sneaking a look at ourselves. Since other people do not have to be dealt with, we can devote all of our energy to watching the only person that remains: our self. The social personality is a tool whose job is to deal with social survival. It has been made to do this, in and by the social context, and is only answerable to that context. To try to use it for examining the self, as we normally use it to examine others, will not work. It may not be the best tool we have to better know ourselves. A hammer is only a fitting tool when combined with nails and wood. To observe the files in our "computer," we need something with a subtler touch. A listening attention is needed, a looking without speaking, an interior silence which observes but does not place value.

Eckhart Tolle gives a good example of the type of attention we need. He asks us to try a little experiment, to close your eyes and say to yourself, "What's my next thought going to be?" then become very alert and wait for this next thought, just as if you were a cat silently watching a mouse hole. What thought is going to pop out? As long as we are in this alert silent watching/listening, no associative thought pattern interferes with our observing. Let's take the experiment a bit further and put ourselves in the context of the hunter or stalker. Our goal is to stalk ourselves. The personality and ego are our game. We wish to observe them, *not observe through them.* Our game is very smart for it knows what we are thinking, even before we think it, for it has had control over us for years, perhaps decades. The only advantage we have is our simple, pure awareness, something the ego lacks. We must become very still and alert, as if we were in a room with a large beast, which can only grab us if we move, feel, or even think. As long as we observe without placing meaning on our observation, we are invisible, and can watch the beast, freely and calmly. If ever the thought comes to us, "Hey, I'm watching myself" or, "Wow, look what I'm doing," we have lost the thread. We are then reacting, not observing. Watch for this "I" thought. If the feeling of "I" and its sense of being the "doer" come into the scene, the listening attention is lost, and you're off the track.

At first we will only be able to watch ourselves during quiet times, such as meditation. While our quarry is relatively still, we are not confused by its movements and are able to hold our attention steady. Later, we can observe when the personality is more active, and we can keep from being thrown off balance. It's good to learn to swim in shallow quiet waters before taking on the waves. Once the basic feel of the listening attention is found, one can progress from observing oneself in quiet times to watching the body and mind as they perform small repetitive tasks. Eventually the awareness will become free enough to observe the self, or "person," in complex actions such as conversation. As we begin to see more and more of ourselves, we gain a certain freedom. Its value does not lie in the modifying of our behavior into a more efficient, flattering form, but simply in becoming free from the hypnotic identification with our pattern. We begin to see we truly do not do and never have. We only observe.

No matter how determined we are to stalk this strange person we call ourselves, we will continue to fall asleep and be swept back into the state of identification. One tool we can make use of to counter this is what might be called "alarm clocks." We create little habits that remind us of our task, which is to watch silently. We place these alarms throughout our day. An example is meditating at a fixed time. The body will become used to this and remind us it's time to turn inward and observe. Another is books or tapes we find to have value. These can serve as alarms by their presence, as well as by their content. One of the best is a group of fellow seekers, who can serve as mirrors of our current state and help snap us back on track. As with anything done with regular routine, these alarms will become less useful with habit, and new ones will be needed.

Another trick is to practice what is called "inner stop." Whenever we sense we are becoming obsessed with a thought pattern, fantasy or habit, whether of anger, self-pity or desire, we can say to ourselves, "Stop!" Just as a loud unexpected noise can stop the conversation in a room, so can this command silence the noise in our head.

One last pointer is what might be called developing 360-degree vision. This is best described as having a two-pronged awareness. One arrow is pointed outwards, towards the relative world and the "person." The other is aimed inward, towards our source. Our quarry, or what we might call the person, can only look out. We have a distinct advantage in being directly connected to that Infinite Silence within and its unlimited patience and wisdom.

Coming to know ourselves eventually crushes the ego, in that we find we are not what we imagined ourselves to be. We begin to see that the person we think we are is purely mechanical, a robot. Honesty and courage will be needed if we are to accept what we see, and perseverance when we find our task difficult and wish to retreat back into imagination. This process of dis-identifying leads to ego-death, as we separate from our pattern. The simple act of clearly seeing the person we were for what it truly is, is enough to bring about its death. We find we have become that which witnesses experience, where before we were experience, creating more and more experiences in an endless mechanical pattern. We are no longer the wily animal we have been tracking, which becomes cleverer with every experience, but instead something free, eternal, and indescribable.

## Cautionary Notes

1.  There is an easy trap to fall into when we first engage in self-obser-vation, and that is to create, or visualize, an observer who observes. We are then back in the same comfortable game we were in, in the first place: that of the personality reacting to the environment in an endless pattern. There is no sentience in mechanical reaction. In describing observation, we are not talking about visualization or imagination but the simple act of looking without reaction, of looking *through* the personality, not *with* it. We have been taught since birth to create and then identify with a separate thing we call ourselves. This reaction pattern continually recreates itself as the person who reacts.

2.  Right Intent. We can only use the listening attention for gaining self-knowledge, knowledge of our own mind. If ambition, ego, or greed comes into play, we have degraded into visualization and are lost. We must want only to scrutinize the self and observe the mind. We must not, and will not be allowed to, take advantage of or gloat over our success. We can take the example of Joseph Sadony to heart. After using his psychic gifts to provide a friend with profitable information in the financial market, he lost his powers for one year to the day. He never again traded his Con-nection for profit.

3. We must have a stable and clear emotional state to succeed. Emotional problems cannot be of a level that spin us out of control. The capacity to walk a straight line, without being sidetracked or continually distracted, is imperative. If we attempt to go into inner silence only to find we are full of unconscious emotional turmoil, then these problems must be dealt with first. To take responsibility for ourselves and to support ourselves, to harbor no excuses; this is the good householder, the level from which we begin. No victims or perpetrators are found in the journey through the valley of death. We must first become a healthy moral animal before we become the hunter, or the beast will hunt us.

### Do Not Fear the Darkness, by Art Ticknor

Dylan Thomas, knowing that his father was dying,
extruded his feelings into a poem that ended with the lines:

> *Do not go gentle into that good night.*
> *Rage, rage against the dying of the light.*

Do they resonate with your own feelings?
There is no need for fear.
My velvet blackness removes all cares,
dispels all vulnerabilities,
terminates all threat
without and within.
Immersed in me emptiness is filled,
longing is finally answered,
permanence is found.
Here, and only here, is love complete,
mother, father, mate, child, friend perfect.
Only when you have lost your self in me
will you find what you've been looking for.

## *Who Am I? by Shawn Nevins*

You don't have to spend your days asking, "Who am I, who am I, who am I ...." Everything you do and everything that happens to you is asking that question for you. It's like the little kid who exasperates his parents by continually asking "why"—"why is the sky blue, why is the grass green, why are we going here?" You are an immensely mysterious creature and a little curiosity about why you do the things you do, will carry you a long way on the spiritual path.

Did you ever watch yourself make a decision? I mean really watch what is going on in your mind. Let us say you don't know what to eat tonight. You think of some options, suddenly a decision is made. Did you decide or did a decision present itself? Were you just the observer of a process?

Did you ever try to catch the first thought of the morning? If you wake up slowly, you will find your mind quite silent. Suddenly there is a thought. Where did it come from? Did you decide it was time to start thinking, or did a process begin without your consent?

Some of our thoughts are obviously automatic. We might say, "It is hot," when the temperature is over 90 degrees. Other thoughts are equally reactive, but harder to trace. For example, we drive to the grocery to buy a chocolate bar when we are depressed, not because we

really want it, but because the sugar gives us pleasure that counteracts the mood. Some people may enter relationships with the opposite sex for the same reasons as buying a candy bar, yet be just as unaware of the real reasons for their so-called decisions.

By examining the reasons for your actions, you are asking, "who am I." By watching your mind to see where decisions occur or thoughts arise, you are asking, "who am I." By simply being curious about your personality and wondering why you have certain likes and dislikes, you are asking, "who am I."

By becoming a watcher of your self, you are engaging in serious spiritual work. You are not that which is observed. You are the observer. If you are truly curious and diligent, you will find you can observe your observing. Here you run into a roadblock—the mind watching the mind.

The mind continues to watch decisions being made, thoughts occurring, and at times watches itself watching. And perhaps, in watching the watching, a great doubt descends as we realize we are watching all that we know, yet feel a hint of something more—beyond our knowing. Beyond knowing, where words fail, where our self fails, where we lose all to become All.

*Appeared in a Pennsylvania newspaper*

# 12: The Mind Turns

## Spiritual Contentment, by Anima Pundeer

*"Is there a different path to spiritual contentment dependent on one's gender?"*

Man and woman are built differently. In my opinion, not taking into account your physical body when you are on a path of self-inquiry is a big mistake. Especially in the initial stages, studying your physical body and how it affects your state of mind is really important. Woman has to take into account her monthly cycle and how it affects her daily perspective of the world depending on what day she is on. Moods affect our worldview, and moods are triggered by the hormones in our body. With changing hormones daily, it is difficult for a woman to realize that her perspective may be changing so frequently. It is easier for a man to follow a discipline and carry it on for a longer period of time than for a woman.

Apart from the physical body, nature has programmed men and women differently. Woman is programmed to ensure that the species doesn't dwindle off. Woman gets more attached and identified with the role she is playing in life. She is the nurturer and has to think of something other than herself first. This is an advantage which makes giving up of ego easier for a woman. Acceptance and surrender come much more easily to a woman than a man. Woman feels much more contentment being of service to others. The path of love and devotion appeals to a woman's psychology much more than the path of Zen. Man is programmed to be a hunter, so he has to fight for everything. Even for Truth.

Nature has made women more intuitive. Woman can use this to her advantage in her search for Self. Whatever aspect you start paying attention to, the inner teacher helps us through that. Be it dream study, insights, writing journals, free association, meditation or intuition, etc.

In today's world, there is a lot of outside pressure as well as inner pressure for women and men to compete against each other. When we are young, we really start to buy into this "you are equal" concept. Especially for women, it creates a lot of pressure to be like men. Any sort of inner peace is not possible in this state of mind. When we get in touch with our true nature, we tend to shed a lot of pretenses and become a more complete woman or man. Working with whatever gender you are resolves a lot of inner as well as outer conflicts. You tend to become more at peace with nature as well as yourself.

Having said that, in the final mile, it really doesn't matter if you have a man's body or a woman's, mind turns completely away from the story. Even the desire for finding the Self burns off. You continue your search for the sake of search. Ego is pretty much shriveled by this time and any desire for self-enhancement is gone completely. Absolute spiritual contentment is no more dependent on your gender.

## *Seek Me First, by Franklin Merrell-Wolff*

The joy is not the end-in-itself to be sought.

Seek Me first, and then My Knowledge and My Joy will also be thine.

Seek Me for My own sake and not for any ulterior motive.
I and I alone am the worthy end of all endeavor.

So lay down all for Me, and My Wealth will be thy wealth, My Power thy power, My Joy thy joy, My Wisdom thy wisdom.

This universe is but a part of My Treasure, and it, with vastly greater Riches, shall be the portion of the Inheritance of all those who come to Me.

Long have ye lingered in the desert of Ignorance.
I desire not thy continued suffering.
Come unto Me. The Way is not so hard.

### *What of Me Will Remain? by Art Ticknor*

*"What of me won't remain when I die—and what of me, if anything, will?"*

I don't doubt that if you could hold that line of thinking in focus, it would do the trick. You would transcend life and death.

An ancient Zenist phrased the above question as: "What is your original face?" Douglas Harding couches his experiments in terms of seeing what it is we're looking out of.

The answer is also that which is self-aware: meaning no subject/object split: meaning no subject.

In my experience, you can glimpse what that is while still identified with the subject-object dimension, the mind. But the glimpse is a shadow of the reality. How then can we comprehend the incomprehensible?

Alfred Pulyan pointed out that "nothing of you remains" when the body dies. That seems to indicate that the lights go out, nothingness prevails, and you're done. If that's the case, then the only meaningful philosophy would be a utilitarian one of optimizing the pleasure-pain mix, or a hedonistic variation such as "eat, drink and be merry" (for tomorrow we die). Fortunately, that's not the case. Nothing of *what you think you are* remains.

Objection: "I don't see that approach as a concrete way of facing mortality, and I think that efforts to try to isolate what would remain after death would be futile because they'd be based on conjecture unless I actually died."

Agreed, thinking about it isn't going to provide a satisfactory conclusion. What is it that we know the least about? The self. In fact, all that can be observed (known) by the mind (knower) is not-self. To isolate what of us might remain after death, we can eliminate anything that can be observed. We can observe the body and, moving inward, we can observe thoughts, feelings, and mental processes. What we run up against is the seemingly impossible task of observing the observer.

When we get frustrated with trying to know the knower, we may opt for a clever out and decide that what we really are is our consciousness. We're awake, and we know we're awake. The problem is that our consciousness doesn't even last through our daily cycle. It comes into existence when we awake, or when we dream, and goes out of existence between those states.

But what may happen, if we continue to try to know ourselves in the face of seeming impossibility, is a glitch in the matrix, a lapse in the space-time continuum, a burning out of a resistance circuit—which frees our identity with the mind and provides the mind with a conscious connection to its unbounded source.

## Poems by Shawn Nevins

I swim in emptiness.
My life dwarfed
by endless possibilities of creation.
Barriers and boundaries have no meaning
here, there, anywhere.

It is the anywhere-ness of this self —
not expanding, but settling
over the landscape
like a paralyzing fog —
that gives a new look to everything old.

I won't be long.
Just let me walk once more
down the sun-lit hill,
feeling like every quiet moment
is my friend
and the world is nothing
but moment after moment.
A last walk with dreams;
with love.

Today lasts forever,
and forever
is speechless before its fate.

In the diffused, muslin light of dream,
buried within the night,
I find my self attending another burial;
arranging the shroud of my long-dead father.

I am in a silent theater
whose edges fade into the unknown.
A baseless creation
save for the moment my hand
brushes against my father's coarse, wavy hair.
This is as real as the last day I touched him,
as real as hands and fathers,
flesh and hair,
dreams and the night that made them.

Inside and outside mean nothing
to the river flowing
through the remains of my destiny.
This walking habit, this phantom self
knows that all is magic,
and words are but symbols
comforting the possessed.

The Truth is scary, but in the End,
When the last blow has fallen,
The last dark secret revealed,
And the last pain has come,
You will find you were a dream.

"Koan"

The entire human race
could wade into this river
today
and it would not rise an inch.
How so?

*Let me tie together:*

I look from a timeless place
with eyes that still dream.

*These bones of thought:*

Don't stay with me,
reveal what I am inside you.

*That rattle inside:*

As the cool of evening descends,
make this place your home.

*This empty place:*

The mind twists Mobius-like.
Truth is a straightening of these contortions.
As a knot is very thin when untangled,
so is life
upon the surface of Reality's timeless depth.

## *Words ... or Experience? by Bob Fergeson*

*"The great danger of the written and spoken word is that you will ingest conclusions without the pain of the growth. You can't do it. It won't work."*
*- Jim Burns*

When I graduated from high school and moved on to a large state university, I received an invaluable lesson in the difference between fact and fantasy, words and Presence. I had been good at the high school curriculum and had been led to believe by my teachers, friends, and proud mother that I was gifted and special, and would be so forever. I had as yet no real knowledge of myself, of what might be called "being." Most of my so-called smarts was made up of memorized facts, a large helping of pride, and an assumed self-confidence based entirely on praise. On entering the larger world of the university, I was soon force-fed the fact that it was all relative, and that an untested life, no matter how inwardly enriched with fantasy, was not much of a life at all.

At about this same time, I encountered the books of Carlos Castaneda. I fell under the spell of his romantic tales of power. Along with several friends, I envisioned myself roaming the desert, wrapped in the fantasy world of allies, magic mushrooms and friendly old sorcerers. We were still not even weaned from our mommies, but in our fantasy realm of no-resistance, of wishful dreaming, we were sure we could do at least as well as the bumbling Carlos, if don Juan would just give us a chance. The months ahead proved to be educational in more ways than one. I flunked out of my first semester, and had to spend a year at a small community college to get my GPA back up. Through a new-found love of the mountains, and a few near disasters there, I also began to realize the difference between being a mountaineer, and dreaming you're one. I was beginning to get a taste of the mechanicalness of my being.

As the years passed, I lost more and more of the attachments to family and upbringing, though never without a shock, but still retained my infatuation with Castaneda's world of magic and freedom. It was not until I had the good fortune to meet a real don Juan, a true "nagual," that things changed. This master was no Indian, Mexican or Hindu, nor Buddhist or Shaman, but a West Virginia native named Richard Rose living a simple life in near anonymity. The difference between him and the don Juan of my fantasies was in his Presence. This man had power. It felt like I was sitting in a room with a live nuclear weapon. I learned more from this than in any and all of the books I'd ever read. I learned what true strength was, the nature of real magic, and that we truly don't learn from books or fantasies. We become through struggle, real experience, and grace. This West Virginia Zen master did not take it easy on me, or anyone who came seeking his help. Instead of just telling us unverifiable tales of power about his teacher through books or lectures, he turned us back on ourselves. We were forced to go within to find an answer. He was all too available and real, maddeningly so.

I had found my don Juan, and he was turning me inside out. I was tested in ways I could never have imagined—and never got to spend a single night in the Mexican desert.

This man had also written books, but he was there to back them up. He made himself available to anyone with a sincere desire to "discover the truth," as he put it, and never charged for his time. He had true being, and by seeing this in him, one could come to know what was possible for oneself, and how to find it. He put no stock in appearances or words, but in action and facts. I saw for the first time the difference between being aware of oneself, and of creating a fantasy and identifying with it.

The search for truth, the journey within, finding our link with the abstract: these are just words until we find the reality they speak of, for ourselves, in ourselves. To place the higher value on the trappings of the adventure and its backgrounds, no matter how exotic, will not get us to loosen our grip on illusion and fantasy. Find a teacher if you can, and don't run away after he throws the first punch. If he's worth finding, he'll raise the grain until you think you're losing your mind. If it was worth his finding you, you will.

## *What Shall I Do When I Meet a Zen Master?*
## *by Alfred Pulyan*

Your problem is the old koan: *What shall I do when I meet a Zen master?* Shall I give him an uppercut, biff him, plug him? Well, if you do, he will either give you a little Judo, if he is a black belt, or, if he is an old man & weak, will politely *transfer you* to another monastery! Occupational hazard! Shall I call him a liar? He will smile & I shall get no further. Besides after knowing him some time I shall see that he is sincere. So? Then the possibility is that he is *self-deceived,* in a state of illusion, mental conjangulation, misunderstanding of subjective experiences etc. etc. Who isn't? After knowing him a little longer I find him keen, sharp, definite, logical, certainly not psychotic, & I begin to say: "Hell. God or no God, give me some of that anyway!" But right *now.* I have just met him. How shall I act? Shall I doubt & yet half hide it, placate him so that he won't run away? If there is A CHANCE that he really is that extraordinary thing, a Buddha, another Jesus, a Lao Tse, an Eckhart, etc. etc. --- then *let us not lose this chance!* So let us cajole a bit, smarm a bit, flatter the old bastard, kiss his venerable posterior, hide our doubts --- The trouble is that the Z.M. knows that one too! Besides *IF HE NEEDS THAT* HE IS STRICTLY NO GOOD, STRICTLY FOR THE BIRDS. Try somewhere else ---

Of course you *could* be just a friend, and friends don't have any communication problem.

Love involves a peculiar unfathomable combination of understanding and misunderstanding. ~ *Diane Arbus*

The key to a successful marriage is not compatibility, love, or anything like that. Rather, the real key is low expectations. ~ *Attributed to Warren Buffett by Hayward Kelly*

If love is the answer, could you please rephrase the question. ~ *Lily Tomlin*

Let us all be happy and live within our means, even if we have to borrow the money to do it with. ~ *Artemus Ward, "Natural History"*

χ

If God dropped acid, would he see people?
If one synchronized swimmer drowns, do the rest drown too?
I went to a bookstore and asked the saleswoman, "Where's the self-help section?" She said if she told me, it would defeat the purpose.
~ *George Carlin*

# 13: The Most Practical Endeavor

*Prologue to The Little Book of Life and Death*
*by Douglas Harding*

κ

*To die is different from*
*What anyone supposes*
*And luckier. ~ Walt Whitman*

It used to be the custom of Zen masters on their deathbeds to compose a *gatha*—a poetic condensation of the insights of a long and dedicated spiritual life, a final comment on life itself and impending death. This essay is my concluding *gatha*. Or rather, it would be if I were a Zen master (or at least a Zen man), and I had obviously come to the very end of my life, and I were writing in verse.

All the same, the composition of something like a secular and prose *gatha* at this time strikes me as not just a useful exercise—a sorting out and taking stock and overall clarification—but a project that's necessary for my own sake if for no others, and very urgent, and in fact long overdue. For already, at seventy-nine, I have lived two or even three times as long as people did on average not so many centuries ago. And of course every new day spent in death row, waiting for the sentence to be carried out, brings that much nearer the moment when I will finally be whisked out of life—perhaps with no warning at all. Into what? Is there a more pressing, more crucial question? It seems to me silly, contemptibly ostrich-like and altogether irresponsible, not to prepare for that moment of truth by asking myself now ... and now ... and now (while the asking is good, and I'm not ill or in pain or drugged or pushed for time) such questions as: "Exactly what is it to live, and then to die? Must I in fact die at all, and—if I must—is this indeed a dead end, the great let-down, the bitter and messy conclusion of the adventure that began so promisingly way back in 1909? And, above all, is it possible to do something right now, first to ensure survival,

141

and second to influence its quality and ensure that it's worthwhile and preferable to annihilation?

Going into these questions as candidly and comprehensively as possible is just about the most practical endeavour of my whole life. Even if no one else were to read my pseudo-*gatha* it demands to be written, clearly and honestly. (I've got to do my utmost to be honest with myself: on this—of all subjects—any suppression of unwelcome evidence, any cheating, would make the whole project a ridiculous waste of time.) I could call it my own highly "personal" and de-mythologized Book of the Dead—not remotely Egyptian or Tibetan of course, or even religious in any ordinary sense, but frankly contemporary and Western and matter-of-fact. For I aim to conduct this enquiry in a spirit that values the most threadbare shred of present *evidence*, the faintest glimmer of first-hand *experience*, the least impulse of humility in the face of the *given*, more highly than libraries full of scriptures and learned commentaries. Here nothing—however uplifting and sacred—is for believing; everything—however mundane—is for trying out and testing. In this life-or-death matter I can afford to take no teaching on trust, to rely on no one's say so—and to neglect no clue. Here at death's door—if nowhere else—I find myself forced to follow the dying Buddha's advice and be a lamp to myself, to take myself to no outside refuge.

This cautious-disrespectful attitude to the religious establishment, to all hallowed authority, is made even more necessary now that (as I shall presently show in some detail) important new empirical evidence on our subject is available. This evidence is of three sorts. The first arises from the skills and the sceptical and far-ranging attitude of modern science, together with some of its actual discoveries—particularly in particle physics. The second arises from recent research into the anecdotes of patients who have been brought back from near death. The third rises from a range of simple experiments I have been using over the past thirty years for investigating our intrinsic nature or First Personhood, techniques for directly perceiving who or what it is here that is conducting these experiments, who or what it is that lives and dies, who or what it is that does nothing of the sort. (A selection of these experiments constitutes the backbone of this book, and—when carried out and not just read about—cannot fail to settle the question of one's nature and destiny.) These three developments—and especially the last—demand that the whole subject be opened out freshly, and that we should start from scratch with as unprejudiced a mind as possible.

Our current resistance to such an investigation, to any candour or realism concerning our own mortality, can scarcely be exaggerated. Witness the popular cult of youth-at-all-costs in the world of advertising and fashion. Witness those communities of old folk dedicated to being "as young as you feel" and to avoiding all reminders of old age, sickness, and death. Witness the newspeak and double-talk of "seventy years young" in place of "seventy years old" and "elderly person" or "senior citizen" in place of "old man," "old woman." Witness the funerary nonsense so tellingly described in Evelyn Waugh's *The Loved One*. Witness Cryonics—the freezing of the newly dead for revival when technology is further developed, thus giving effect to the view that "death is an imposition on the human race, and no longer acceptable."[1] Witness the cultists who seriously maintain that death is unnecessary and unnatural, and we can choose to live as long as we wish. How unlike the veneration of old age and the preoccupation with death and the hereafter which are such marked features of some great cultures! And again, what a contrast with the *memento mori* (remember you must die) of earlier centuries of our own civilization—its human skulls carved on tombstones and displayed on mantelpieces, its countless engravings

---

[1] Alan Harrington, *The Immortalist: An Approach to the Engineering of Man's Divinity*, New York, Random House, 1969.

143

and paintings confronting the living with the grim spectacle of Death the Reaper and the imagined sequel!

Were our ancestors just morbid? Rather it is we, with our pathetic Nelson's-eye for the least escapable fact of our life—its end—who are morbid. Only in part is our wilful blindness offset, at a less popular level, by modern depth-psychology: for instance, by the view that there is just one real but well-concealed terror—the fear of death—from which our many conscious fears all derive. The lesson for me is plain: attack fear at its root. Test the bold claim of the Sufi master Attar, "The only remedy for death (and the fear it generates) is to look it constantly in the face."

And for sure we don't lack our very own uniquely powerful *memento mori*—namely our all too justified anxiety about the possibility or probability of nuclear war followed by a nuclear winter, the species' mass suicide. We are all being forced to admit that we live precariously, in the Valley of the Shadow of Death.

However, the death that comes to you and me anyway—sooner or later—is never experienced as a mass event: but only by *this* solitary one: I mean, by the First Person Singular, present tense, never by second or third persons as such. In short, by oneself alone with oneself. Inevitably my death, and this preview of it, is the most personal and private adventure imaginable. And of course, just because of this unique and inescapable intimacy, it is universal, everyone's adventure—which is why I'm inviting you, my reader, to join me now in this enquiry.

Before we make a start, let's conclude these preliminary observations with a warning and a promise from a famous Buddhist text, the *Dhammapada:* "Vigilance is the path of immortality, heedlessness the path to death. The vigilant do not die, but the heedless are already like the dead." This assertion, though it proves nothing at all, should encourage us to give to this matter all the care, truthfulness, open-mindedness, and attention of which we are capable.

## *Poems by Art Ticknor*

I am pursuing you with relentless love,
awaiting your return with infinite patience,
ready to enfold you in the boundless love of true identity.

When you've suffered long enough
with your dreams of temporal satisfaction,
turn around and come home.

I am always waiting to guide you
since I know you've lost your way.
I am always right behind you.

❧

*Heaven*
neither travels ahead
nor lags behind
but is always with you.

Simply remove the barriers,
and you're there.
The barriers have no heft
being nothing other than beliefs.

Beliefs of being right or being wrong
are intermediate barriers.
Beliefs of being something
are the final barriers.

Heaven is the place
of no place, no time.
No thing has ever made it through
the gate between thingland and heaven.

❧

"Hearing"

O incomprehensible not-twoness,
Whose music is the silent hum upon which the ears and the sound
waves of the universe ride,
Where within thee is hearing, where the phantom hearer?

145

## *Asceticism, by Shawn Nevins*

Ascetics are the extreme athletes of the spiritual search—the people who fast for days at a time, pray without sleeping, wear hair shirts and live in desert huts, sleep in unheated rooms on beds of nails, and a hundred other variations on the theme of controlling and purifying the body. The ascetic looks upon the body as a barrier to spiritual knowledge, or he believes that his sacrifices will draw the blessings of God. This is an ancient tradition with many sad extremes, yet it has a basis in truth. The body is not so much a barrier to spiritual knowledge as it is a tool we use poorly. Ascetic practice sharpens the body and mind, expanding our ability to act effectively. The modern seeker of self-definition who scoffs at asceticism may be most in need of this experiment.

The truth is that our lives are a mix of desires. We want a piece of sugary cake, yet want to lose weight. This simple conflict illustrates a body that wants, under the cover of pleasure, fuel in the form of sugar and fat. At the same time, we want to stay thin in order to attract a mate and keep the body healthy. The modern man's solution is to indulge all these wants and declare the need for a balanced life. Such a balance is akin to trying to keep everyone (i.e. every facet of the self) happy all the time. The result is temporarily contented mediocrity.

Asceticism is self-denial for the purpose of redirection of personal energy. By denying an aspect of your self, you test to see its permanence. If you refuse to eat cake for a month, and discover that desire fades, then you eliminate a less true facet of your self. You can ignore the voice that calls for cake and concentrate your energy on more important matters. You gain a measure of freedom.

Asceticism is not simply the denial of pleasure. Nor is it the substitution of pain for pleasure. The experience of pleasure is not a detriment to the spiritual path and self-induced agonies are not tickets to heaven. It is our many obsessions that are a detriment to success. Your obsession must be with self-definition if you wish to assuage your deepest desire.

Success in the quest for self-definition requires a commitment of your mind and body. There are many desires competing for a finite amount of energy and you must discover which are necessary (e.g., the need for basic food), which can be eliminated (e.g., the need to get drunk), and which can be lessened (e.g., the need for money). Success

will be determined by the amount of energy (time, desire, effort) you bring to bear on the question, "Who are you?"

Asceticism will clarify your desires. Through this artificial creation of adversity, you will discover what you never truly needed. As you come closer to identifying your true desires, you come closer to following your bliss. Following your bliss, following your heart, will lead you home.

There is another more subtle value of asceticism. A sacrifice is a statement of your intent. It is saying to whatever may be listening that you are serious, that you are willing to make an intimate sacrifice. Such a statement changes who you are.

Although wearing hair shirts is out of fashion, there are numerous ascetic practices. I engaged in practices such as: limiting sleep, fasting, eliminating sugar and spices, isolation, not talking, no alcohol, no television or other media, and celibacy. For some, an ascetic practice could be no online chat rooms for a week. There are individual distractions and they change over time. Don't doom your self by taking on numerous practices simultaneously. If you stumble in your practice, simply determine to try again and do a little better. Gradually wean your self, if need be. The end result will be a balance of desires, but a balance obtained within the over-riding goal of the desire for self-definition.

## *The Sculptor, by Gary Harmon*

As the sculptor
To the delight of his heart
Molds the clay,
So you can create
To the splendor of your nature
Your own future.

As the logger
Cuts a path
Through the thick forest,
So can you slice your passageway
Though this turmoil of suffering,
An obvious corridor
To your freedom from sorrows,
To everlasting contentment.

As for a moment
The mysterious mountains
Are concealed by the passing mists,
So are you also anonymous,
In the darkness
Of your own origin.
The fruit of the seed that was planted
Shall saddle you.

Heaven and Hell
Are words
To frighten you into correct action;
But heaven and hell, neither one does exist.
Only the seeds of your own actions
Shall bring into being
The blossoming that is longed for.

As the author of images
Carves the human shape
Out of granite,
So out of the rock
Of your own occurrence,
Find eternal happiness.

Your life is death;
Death is a rebirth.
Contented is the one
Who is beyond the grasp
Of these imposed limitations.

## Going Within, by Bob Cergol

Richard Rose writes in his booklet on meditation:

> The ultimate aim of meditation is to go within. Going within means to find Reality by finding the Real part of ourselves. It does not mean merely playing around inside the head with random observations which we have discussed as being important to understanding the natural mechanism of man's mind.

> When we begin to meditate in the attempt to go within we should simply observe our self. We cannot really do it simply. It is a very profound task or attempt.

He also writes in that booklet of the levels of meditation, of which "Going Within" is the 4th level. The instruction given is: "Employ whatever necessary."

What does it mean to "go within"?

It's not a place, and you don't really "go" anywhere. It refers to the direction of one's attention.

What is it that you do to "go within"?

Life is basically an experience. Experience is a continuous stream. We can categorize our experience as "inner" and "outer." Inner experience refers to the totality of our individual reaction to outer experience—and on another level to inner experience itself in a spiraling, even "tail-chasing" process so the line between inner and outer is blurred—and ultimately may prove to be a false distinction, i.e. all experience is external....

Going within means a shift in the object of seeing or listening, of one's attention from the perceptions and events swirling around us to the seeing or listening to our reactions to life's experiences.

What determines those reactions?

We engage ceaselessly in evaluating whether our sense of self is affirmed or diminished. The former is pleasure. The latter is pain.

Which reaction is dominant for you? What is its source?

What fills your attention most of the time?

I believe that fear of death develops in concert with the development of identity, for the simple reason that intellectually we know that the body is mortal and therefore cannot be the vehicle that will ensure survival of that identity. The escape mechanism is to disassociate from the body, place oneself anterior to it and take possession of it, as it were. But since there is no hard proof, there is this core knowledge of the lie, and our lives become an incessant, doomed-to-fail effort at proving the independent existence of that identity by attempting to magnify it through experience.

What is the motivation for shifting your attention away from external experience to look at inner experience? Or said another way, what motivates you to examine what is occupying your attention?

The primary motivation is whenever experience diminishes the sense of self. It is not really motivation since the shift is a reaction. If looking at the internal experience of reaction is painful, the automatic reaction is to shift the attention away either by engaging in rationalizing analysis or by engaging in alternative mental or physical activity.

What result do you expect from "going within" as you conceive it?

## Consciousness versus Awareness: definitions

The dictionary defines the words "consciousness" and "awareness" as synonyms, and each word is used in the definition for the other. The definition for both words depends on there being an object to which consciousness or awareness applies. This implies that there must be a subject who possesses the attribute of consciousness. One is either conscious of something or not. In this sense the words are verbs and denote action by an individual being—even if that action is itself either automatic—or an unconscious action!

Students of the esoteric have this concept that "God" or the "Source" is pure "awareness." They conceive this awareness to be a possession or attribute of God's, just as they perceive it to be an attribute or possession of their own self—or one that can be acquired. Realization is conceived as adding god-like awareness or consciousness to this same personal self. This all stems from an egocentric point of reference that places their ego anterior to everything else. Seekers of enlightenment have this idea that they will become god-like, or one with god, or attain this god-like awareness, and so there is the presumption of personal immortality and eternal ego consciousness.

### Let's see how this would apply to God, Supreme Being or Transcendental Awareness:

- ◆ What is the object of this consciousness or awareness? What is God aware of?
- ◆ If God's awareness is without object then, how is God alive according to our concept of being? Does God know that he's alive?
- ◆ Does the knowledge of "being alive" require an identity? Would you be alive without your identity?—Without your body? Without your mind? Without—YOU!?
- ◆ If God is all-knowing, what does he think about?
- ◆ If God is beyond all thought, what occupies his attention?
- ◆ If God is the object of his own attention, how long is God's attention span?
- ◆ If God is beyond time and exists eternally, then how could God not be eternally bored with himself?
- ◆ If you believe in your own immortality, or even the possibility, what will the object of your attention be for eternity?
- ◆ Can you imagine yourself, your identity with all its history, as the object of your consciousness for eternity—with no ability to alter that history? Is that realization?—Or the definition of Hell?

I distinguish between the two words *consciousness* and *awareness*.

For me, consciousness is personal and temporary; awareness is impersonal and timeless. Consciousness is the experience of individuality, and awareness is that which powers it. The "experience of individuality" is motion on a background of immobility—a whisper that cannot alter or penetrate the silence. Consciousness is a point. Consciousness is the point at which the un-manifested intersects the manifested. Awareness is boundless.

Awareness is consciousness without an object, unless you wish to say that awareness is its own object.

How then does an individual become aware of that which is anterior to that individual? The question seems a contradiction—indeed a Koan!

The short answer is by "abandoning the ego-centric position"—another paradox. The verb *abandon* implies action by the ego, which action itself would reinforce the supremacy of the ego's position. Therefore it is said that the ego is taken from you or dropped. When one "gives up" or "expires" it is not a voluntary action but a spontaneous acceptance or natural consequence....

The process is negative or subtractive. *The end result is not created by the process.*

## TWO MEDITATION EXERCISES:

Superficial "Going Within"—skirting with loss of self—and resistance.... (Looking at self-dissatisfaction in a specific instance.)

Focus your attention on that which bothers you the most about yourself. What troubles you more than anything else? (It is that which is wrong about yourself—that which hinders you from attaining the fullness of life that you crave.)

This is not "going within." This is focusing the attention on one's reactions to external experience. This reaction comprises one's internal experience. It's like a "parallel universe" or dream world that is evoked by external experience.

Real "Going Within"—acceptance of what is.... (Looking at the self directly.)

Focus your attention on what it feels like right at this moment to be you—to exist as you. You have to do this gently. You cannot strain to focus the attention in this fashion. You need only to just notice your sense of self and then gently notice how does it feel to exist as this identity this moment.—Perhaps you notice a certain positive or negative feeling that accompanies your self-existence.

How strong is the sense of existence as you?

This is a crude attempt to illustrate my point that: Self-dissatisfaction is merely the kindling to light a fire that must ultimately consume you. You must get to a point where the looking inward is automatic, and there is either not much reaction to what you see—or, if there is strong reaction, there is simultaneously a detachment from and acceptance of the reaction—just as if it's merely another part of the experience you've had to contend with all along anyway, and it's no longer of much value to you.

Note: For years my meditations were all about me—my problems, my feelings, becoming free of myself. There was much I didn't like about myself, and I'd lost track of it all and just plain felt bad, inferior to others. It was only after this had burnt itself out—with some help perhaps from looking at it—that I began to look at the world outside myself. And when this happened, I began receding from it—automatically.

*From a presentation made at the July 2003 TAT meeting.*

## *Commentary on Going Within, by Bob Cergol*

One thing I'd like to clarify is that the "Meditation type 1" description [in the preceding article] sounds as though I'm completely dismissing, even recommending against, the practice of looking at what troubles oneself. This is not what I think. Relative to true "going within" it is superficial—scratching the surface—but it is still necessary in the beginning and, I suspect, is the beginning point for everyone. It's what starts the reversal process in the focus of one's attention. Moving the attention in a direction away from the most outward experience and instead toward the source of that experience. The degree to which people develop strategies to counter this reversal, i.e. "looking away," might be a fundamental, if not ultimate, distinction among them, though I don't know how to account for this serendipity. I wonder what percentage of people are able to keep up this avoidance strategy right into their own death experience. For some people it takes a lifetime to "retraverse this projected ray." We've read of others, Ramana Maharshi for one, who did so in a very short time. One thing I've come to appreciate is how the turbulence of experience blankets Awareness like a dense fog.

Rose once responded, "Well it dims and brightens, that's about the best way I can tell you," to a question about his realization: "Do you experience this awareness of yourself now, or is it something that the person loses when he comes back?" (*Direct-Mind Experience*, p. 104). But the Absolute cannot exist in degrees, manifest in degrees or be experienced in degrees. (Remember Pulyan's comment [in correspondence with Richard Rose] that "while I can imagine having more of what I've got, there are no degrees!" What then was he referring to that he could have more of?)

The realization of one's being doesn't brighten and dim—rather, the turbulence of mind slows or hastens like a fog obscuring the view of the world. The mind must be emptied. Experience fills the mind. The self that people take themselves to be arises in the mind—and exists only on the level of experience. The mind must be emptied, but no amount of effort will completely empty it because the final content is the experience of individuality—of identity—and that identity did not generate itself, but it fights mightily to affirm itself, and the fight generates more experience. Beyond this mind-content is true Being.

It took 25 years (more or less) for my mind to become emptied. Now it takes anywhere from zero to five minutes for me to shake off the fog that the experience of my mundane life generates as I allow myself to live it. But I am not doing anything. I am not re-establishing contact. I am not causing Awareness to brighten for "me." Everyone has exactly the same "brightness" of Awareness. The difference lies in the density of the fog enshrouding it. As the fog lifts, you go with it. What's left is what's real. There is an experience that accompanies this, an echo of the real in the field of mind, and it is that which dims and brightens for me. After you've looked at the content of your mind for so long that you just cannot look at it any more, that content ceases to be the object of your attention. But the looking doesn't stop at that point! It's the same with dreams. Upon waking you may stare at the dream you just had—and stare until, out of exasperation at unraveling and discerning the meaning of the dream's content, you just give up, or just grow weary. At that point the staring coasts and something remains as its object. This something that remains is very important and real—and yet it is not "there." Then you wake up and start your day and perhaps pause to meditate and stare some more.

This is the paradox of effort and effortlessness. Realization only occurs when one stops trying. But in order to see, one must first look!

Before you can reach this state of effortless looking, you must make great efforts to look! Otherwise, the endless swirl of experience will fill your mind and sweep you away.

When all of the content of consciousness melts away, I am what remains.

## Going Within: The Object of Attention, by Bob Cergol

*The "Object of Attention" chart below was used in Bob's July 2003 TAT meeting presentation. Some additional commentary follows.*

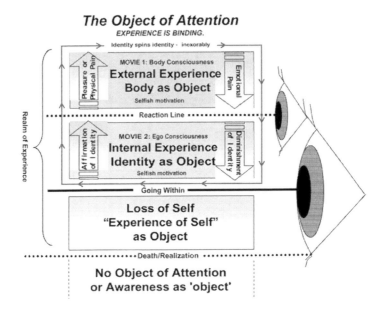

The two "experience" boxes comprise two movies running concurrently at all times. The "Internal Experience" or movie-2 runs in concert with movie-1, which is "External Experience / Body as the object of attention." The "Identity spins identity" cycle occurs around the reaction line between these two in the diagram. The "reaction line" has "hair-trigger" sensitivity.

Affirmation of the self through experience is doomed to fail because that which is not real cannot be made real by more of that which generates the illusion in the first place. (We are left unsatisfied, and the nagging feeling of not being truly affirmed remains.) It is a foregone conclusion that it will lead to pain and diminishment of such a self. Life itself does that to us as we are all in the process of dying. The reaction line and arrows depict how the ego does not want to look at or accept diminishment and so deflects—"spins"—such painful and diminishing experiences into affirmations. And so people wander mesmerized, outwardly, lacking in any real self-awareness.

To break through the "Going Within" line requires dispassionate, detached, pure looking at experience—without spinning it. I think this is the surest way to achieve the "Who/What Am I?" meditation. It is an oblique way. It is how the between-ness of effort / no-effort is achieved, which is required for the jump to "experience of self" becoming the object of the attention. Here the witnessing point of reference transcends selfish motivation and the body-identity. I think for many, direct attempts to meditate on "Who Am I?" result in a form of sleep or hypnosis with the sense of identity firmly and safely anchored in the background. The meditation becomes an affirming experience for this ego-consciousness, when what is required is for transcendence of that ego-consciousness, i.e., "loss of self." (We need to discover what we are not, as opposed to continued weaving and believing.)

Experience is binding, and the attention is held captive by experience—indeed we derive our sense of personal existence from it—and the ingrained habit is to keep spinning it to reinforce the reality of that personal existence. It therefore makes perfect sense that focusing one's attention on experiences that afflict the sense of self is a catalyst for breaking that cycle and truly going within.

When the "experience of self" is the object of the attention, it is still within the realm of experience, but that experience is now fragile and subject to being seen as unreal—even dreamlike. But the viewpoint is still egocentric and identity-based. The identity is now truly threatened and at risk because aspects that comprise it are seen as having no substance. This inevitably leads the attention to looking towards the source from which that entire sense of self-existence emanates.

With this "going within," the stage is then set—the mind softened up—for the final acceptance of Reality, and therefore the "accident" can happen: one is open and receptive to what previously one could never see, since one will not see that which one, in advance, will not accept.

# 14: The Fact of Who You Are

## *On Dream Study, by Jim Burns*

There is a free association part of the mind that is like a citizen's band scanner, constantly going up and down the channels. Your inner mind is constantly trying to get your outer self aware of what's going on within yourself until you've answered to that need. It keeps throwing balls over the fence. As you drive down the road your mind will constantly pick out this fence, or that tree, or this sign. You're accustomed to it and assume that everyone else's mind does the same thing. If you analyzed why you pick this or that to see out of everything that is available, there is a definite reason and pattern to it. It follows very closely the things that come in ordinary dreaming (which is another method of throwing balls over the fence). The dream-maker uses these things in waking life. They are attempts to guide you to what in you is unfulfilled.

When I was young I learned that dreams were the source of all necessary information. It's good to go to sleep slowly and to wake up slowly. If you have a nagging dream, just lie in bed and be quiet. Try and be conscious of no-thing, which is different than nothing. Just let it come to you. All the pictography of the dream is an attempt by the inner stage master to throw things over the fence to key you in to what is happening in your insides. Through dreams you can repair the bridge to the inner self and again become a whole person.

Realizing something in a dream isn't enough; you have to become aware of it in the waking state. When I was good at dreams, several times I was able to go deep inside myself and hear the dream and actually be able to see it, and get a person to repeat what they said time after time until I was able to re-experience the dream. In interpreting my dreams, what I would do when I woke up was to go all the way back to the crossover state. The feelings that the dreams elicit are the things that tell you what the dream means, so you have to be able to go right back into it. Whatever the same feelings are that would occur to you when you are awake, is what the dream is trying to get to. The real point in dreams is to get it to come back so clearly that you get all the feelings as they went by.

When you are doing what your soul wants to do, you'll have so much energy you won't know what to do with it. If it is in the mental realm, you have to balance it by doing something physical to bring the body chemistry back into equilibrium. You will start head tripping if you don't. You have to do something physical to bring yourself back down. Locations have something to do with this also. There's such a thing as not being able to be your true self in certain locations or places associated with negative experiences. In dreams you go to the locations or settings where you can be your true self.

Your inner side is always trying to bring these things to your attention. Paranoia is another method, and is not delusion but your inner mind trying to get you to pay attention to something, and it won't stop until you bite the bullet. Hearing voices is another example. Voices are a person's own self, and if you could demonstrate that, it would be the end of voices. I know. I've been down that road.

## *Poems by Shawn Nevins*

Look with attention.
Be honest about what you see.
Ignore what is temporary.
Probe deeper into what seems real.

❧

Lying here I see
the empty, blue sky
is my heart.
Distance dissolved,
I pour out of my self
into everywhere.

❧

It is a matter of mistakes:
A man and woman
sitting across a table
thinking, hoping
that somehow
flesh will bridge this gap,
this gulf
between two shells.
Hard shells, convoluted and worn,
yet with the same whispered calling inside.

❧

Always we are moments away from drowning –

Our conceptions like frantic paddling.
I stopped dreaming a long time ago
And strove to see only what was there.
I found one part of me busy
And another still.

Like the hunter who walks silently,
I knew the answer was in stillness,
While not in inaction.

As peace is not in the cellar,
But in the eye of the storm.

My life opened in the darkness
like a morning glory,
though I found no color inside,
only the giving of my self
to an emptiness that abounds.

My self is burning,
drawn by gravity into this atmosphere,
leaving a trail of living
that fades,
even as I return
to my origin.

My steps are not taken by me,
Yet I walk.
I will fall like any man,
Yet I am untouched.
On the night of your death
I will shed tears meant for that night alone.
My pain is that of a man who is no more,
Whose steps are like breezes —
Purposeful and empty.

## *Gauging Realization in Oneself and Others, by Bob Cergol*

Most of us have observed in some fashion the capacity for self-delusion in others, and any serious practitioner of self-inquiry has also observed—often with surprise and distress—examples of self-delusion in their own life. So it is understandable that the question arises of how does one know the degree of realization (or delusion) in oneself or another.

My attempt to answer, or rather comment on, these questions is based on defining the spiritual path as one's journey to discovering who and what one ultimately is, i.e. self-definition. The spiritual search ends in the discovery of what remains when all that is not your true Being is taken away. You do not willfully shed the false, so the words "taken away" are used deliberately. You look, and when you are ready to accept that which prevents you from seeing (fear), the false falls away. Looking beyond the very core of what you take yourself to be requires a shock or accident concurrent with your intense, unselfish looking.

No matter how often individuals have heard the term "reverse vector" applied to the search or that the spiritual path is subtractive, the automatic and unconscious direction of their mind—of their very individuality—is additive. Every experience results in a reaction of instantaneous interpretation that the experience affirms and magnifies their individuality, or denies and diminishes that individuality.

Such a mentality is in a very poor position for evaluating its own progress on the path, let alone the attainment of another.

I've written somewhere else that one cannot really lie to oneself, that one only looks away from the truth because one is not ready to accept it. In our heart we know the difference. We have only to look in earnest. In this sense, the spiritual path is a journey of acceptance and a willingness to have a look, directly and honestly, at just who and what we really are—and are not—and it takes time, for it is really the process of dying—and who willingly rushes to embrace that?

Nisargadatta was quoted as saying: "He who knows himself has no doubts about it. Nor does he care whether others recognize his state or not."

Someone who does not know themselves is in no position to judge the spiritual attainment of another. The best they can hope for is to make an accurate intuitional assessment of that person's sincerity, friendship and capacity to help them in their search. The reliability of their intuition is dependent in large measure on the degree to which they know themselves and can be unselfishly honest with themselves. Their evaluation, either way, of the other person has no bearing on the fact of the other person's state. Therefore it is more important that one look at oneself than to be preoccupied with proving or disproving the status of another and whether they are self-deluded or not.

There is an underlying assumption, held by convention, that self-realization automatically makes of the person both a teacher and some sort of epic character whose entire life thereafter takes on epic proportions. Along with this comes a whole laundry list of personality traits and behaviors that are applied as a test of whether someone is self-realized or not. These assumptions are erroneous and come from a mentality that believes spiritual realization somehow increases the individual.

The individual who was the trigger for Richard Rose's realization was not even an active seeker, let alone a realized teacher, so one should not equate efficacy in evoking realization in one's self with the state of self-realization in another or rule out the value that any specific individual may have to you in your attempts to see yourself clearly.

Richard Rose once told me: "Enlightenment doesn't change the fact of who you are in the world. A whoremaster could realize the Absolute, after which he'd still be a whoremaster. Oh, I ain't saying he'd have the same attachment to being that character as before. In Zen you hear that before Enlightenment the hills are hills and the valleys are valleys; in enlightenment the hills are no longer hills and the valleys are no longer valleys; then after enlightenment the hills are once again hills and the valleys are once again valleys." (Note: To argue that this saying limits enlightenment to a mere experience in time is to miss entirely the point that this saying makes.)

Another common assumption is that self-realization must bring happiness and joy—even physical health. This comes in part from the use of the word Bliss in many Eastern writings. Apparently, the Indian term translated as "bliss" in English does not mean "intense, unbroken, happiness" as I think is the most common interpretation. From the context I see it used in, I conclude it means a state that is beyond both joy and sorrow—a state that is unaffected by the swirl of relative experience and its accompanying emotions. Bliss would be equanimity at one's core—the result of the knowledge of one's true Source and the result of both knowing and experiencing oneself to BE that Source—even all the while experiencing the tumult of one's life's circumstances (karma) and the emotional reactions that belong to the personality and the body. (The Zen teacher Pulyan, in response to a question regarding what his system was, replied: "You want a process that 'enhances.' What does that mean—gives you joy & pleasure. This will NOT!")

Having said all this, I feel comfortable in laying out these characteristics of someone who has realized their true nature, beyond which I don't think one can generalize.

1.  They have witnessed and experienced their own non-existence and so have solved the problem of life and death in regards to themselves.

    Not merely as a discursive conclusion—though I acknowledge that such tail-chasing could precede and precipitate a final realization.

164

In that case, I would say that any such discursive thought process was merely the experience—not the cause—that coincided with the process by which the individual's awareness disassociated from that which was not the Self. When the body-mind dies and is dissipated, when motion which is all of the content of consciousness ceases, something remains. It is No-thing—but the word "nothing" connotes absence and denial, and that which remains is quite real—the only real being—alive but beyond life and death—and is all that is. Hence, Richard Rose also said that it was Everything. The dreamer, by virtue of the very nature of his source, has seen his dream nature. This seeing itself is but a reflection of the Source, for the Source doesn't see or hear—it simply IS.

2.  They live with two simultaneous points of reference.

One point of reference is relative, which I would describe as awareness-illuminated experience; the other is absolute and impersonal and beyond experience, i.e., awareness independent of any object. The former is the point of reference of individuality that has peered back through the mind, back through individual consciousness, and in doing so left that individuality behind, revealing a different point of reference that is anterior to that individual and from which individuality itself is witnessed as an experience—an event, a movement apart from eternal stillness. Paradoxically, only the latter point of reference is real. Language breaks down because such expressions always suggest or inject the notion of the personal, i.e., an individual experiencing or witnessing. In reality the personal only exists as a dream, and the dream character has an experience of realization and lives in that experience; all the while there is a persistent background of impersonal awareness, an abiding sense of That which alone is real and in which the personal is a fleeting reflection. (Pulyan replied to a question on this very subject: "This is a paradox to make the angels weep!! Since you *are* 'God' & *nothing else* it is God realizing himself in this time-space episode.")

3.  They are permanently changed.

This change is not necessarily visible to others. No matter how they live their lives and what happens to them, there is a perspective that cannot be lost. I call this perspective "seeing from the other side," and it is the background of all their experience. The quality of their awareness is changed—not their Being, since that which they truly are is beyond change. The reaction of the personality to this change in awareness is highly varied and, for me, explains the wide divergence of vocabulary and actions among those who have written convincingly about their realization.

Nisargadatta provides us this succinct description of Self-Realization: "… A state of pure witnessing, detached awareness, passionless and wordless. It is like space, unaffected by whatever it contains. Bodily and mental troubles do not reach it—they are outside 'there'—while the witness is always 'here.' "

There is no doubt in one when this witnessing occurs as to its finality—though one may be dumbstruck and poorly equipped for explaining it. There may even be a period of adjustment for the personality. It is unexpected—and these words do not prepare you for it no matter how much you might think you understand them, no matter how well you have learned the language of the literature—so I see little chance for enduring self-delusion here by him who is honest with himself. One would have to ignore the fact of their own mortality throughout their entire life and the question it presents them—and one day will present them one final time: "Who am I?" and "What is this existence?" and "What comprises me?" and "What remains when body and mind perish and are dissipated?"

### O Come All Ye Faithful, by Art Ticknor

There are those who have faith in Me
> but aren't good listeners.

And there are those who don't have faith in Me
> and refuse to hear Me.

Are you unsure of what direction to take,
> what option to choose?

I am the path to all that life has to offer,
> but you don't remember Me.

Thus speaks your inner self,
> the Love and the Answer that you're looking for.

## Fact and Fantasy, by Bob Fergeson

*Zen is "Walk, don't wobble."*
*- Richard Rose*

Many of us go through life enamored of ourselves to the point of not really knowing where we are headed or why. We refuse to question our decisions in any meaningful way, and only after a severe shock or trauma will we ever admit we may not have been what we thought. One of the dominant features of many seekers of truth is a feeling of superiority which tends to blind the student to his own true life pattern. In other words, we live in our heads, safely hidden from the facts of our real existence.

If we are lucky enough to be clobbered into wakefulness and the truth of our life through trauma or necessity (I have no interest in speaking to those who are convinced they are "ripe souls," needing only to wait in idleness for their coming release), we may find we have been blind to something Richard Rose called our "fact-status." For example, when I first entered university, I was so convinced of my own superiority that I never thought of cracking a book, never bothered to show up for class or take notice of the declining state of my health and mind. After flunking out my first semester, becoming hooked on drugs, and letting my teeth nearly rot, I was forced to re-evaluate my thinking. My fact-status could no longer be ignored, no matter how far I hid in inner fantasy.

The above pattern of self-conflict, while a bit extreme, illustrates the gap between our false image of ourselves and our fact-status. We are continually knocked off balance by this conflict, and instead of facing the truth about ourselves and acting accordingly, many of us simply regroup, re-invent, and continue to live *as if* the story in our heads were true. The ego refuses to see anything wrong about itself, thus denying that which asserts otherwise, fact or not. We continue to be lulled asleep. Falling off the log into the stream of unconsciousness, we are shocked awake and climb back up, only to succumb again to the ego's song of distraction and desire, wobble off balance, and again take the plunge. This continued stumbling between ego-fantasy and the shock of the facts eats up our time and energy. We can keep up the game when we are young, for a while, but sooner or later we tire, become isolated, defensive, and begin to crystallize. Any hope of finding something beyond the ego fades as the ego becomes all.

The above may sound hopeless. But balance can be obtained if we persevere, learning from our mistakes and those who have gone before us. Rose called the process of using what uses us "milk from thorns." By recognizing the ability of our own mind to delude itself, we can hopefully set up a system of checks and balances to insure that our idea of ourselves is, at least, somewhat related to the facts. This fact-checking can be brought about in many ways: through honest friends and family, co-workers and colleagues. Another one is intuition, learning to listen to the small voice within. Most importantly, we can become more aware by learning to be honest in truly observing ourselves. This use of self-observation, which might be called the opposite of rationalization, is spoken of by every serious system of finding spiritual truth.

Now, there are some of us who say, "Why bother with observing myself, when the great teachers recommend inquiring directly within for the absolute?" To find the truth, or absolute, one needs to be a true vector of inquiry. The above examples of how we are not this true vector, or stable inquirer, show the myriad paths of fantasy in which we become entangled. Let us not presuppose ourselves to be something we are manifestly not. A quick check of our fact-status will show us how we are ready, willing and able to be distracted from inner inquiry at the drop of a hat or wink of an eye. Learning to walk a straight line, upright and somewhat mentally sober, would be a good first step. Developing one-pointedness of mind first, we then turn this beam upon ourselves, now knowing the difference between fact and self-created fiction. We are beginning to have a sense of balance through wielding the sword of discernment.

By developing and using this power of discrimination on our own minds, we come to see how and where the ability to fool ourselves originates. We come to know our minds, and thus become objective or anterior to them. Through this process of separation from our former "self," and through a growing acceptance of our fact-status (things as they are), we find we have been practicing what may be called a practical form of self-inquiry combined with surrender, and have made real progress. When we look back on the delusions we so readily accepted and projected, we have to laugh at ourselves and our previous stumblings about. The value of this progress is not in that we have found reality but in that we have become better able to discern the real from

the unreal, and thus have increased our odds of knowing reality if we ever do happen to bump into it. In the words of Richard Rose, "We must desire the Truth, and have a capacity for it else we could not receive it even if it came to us by accident." By learning to walk, not wobble, we keep from continually falling off the log of discernment before we get to the other shore. We become painfully aware of the games we insist on playing, and the fears we harbor, and realize we might not desire the truth about ourselves as much as we thought. We begin to see our true inner motivations, heretofore unconscious, and thus have the beginning possibility of real self-inquiry through a stable mind, and real surrender through acceptance of truth.

*Now this may be rather trivial, but I thought it was very illustrative for skeptics of how programmed they are—body and mind. After trying this exercise, imagine how much more easily thoughts move in tandem with the body. ~ Bob Cergol*

While sitting at your desk, lift your right foot off the floor and make clockwise circles. Now, while doing this, draw the number "6" in the air with your right hand. Your foot will change direction, and there's nothing you can do about it.

*Kind of cool. If I go really slow, I can make both motions. Also, if I quickly sign the number six. In the first method, I think the brain is rapidly shifting from one task to the next. In the later, I may be relying on something like "muscle memory" to make the number. Also neat to try using the left hand and foot. Ahhh, also try it using opposite hands and feet—can definitely tell there is separation between the halves of the brain. Even more illustrative of my programming is the fact that I'm sitting here doing what you suggested. ~ Shawn Nevins*

# 15: Yearning

## *Developing Intuition, by Shawn Nevins*

It has been said before—a person without intuition is lost. They will fall prey to those who use elegant words but have no heart or substance. At best, they will stumble upon a true teacher, but be unable to adapt that teaching to their needs. The best spiritual teaching is not a map. Rather, the best teaching tells you how to create a map by using your common sense (logic) and horse sense (intuition).

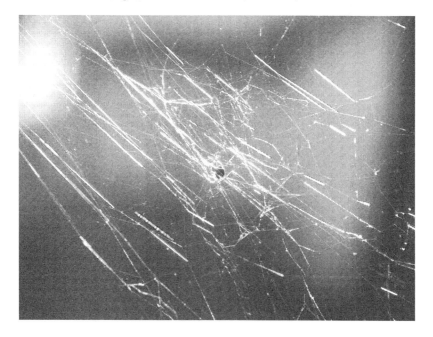

One must realize the need to improve the intuition. The mind is our tool in spiritual research. Within mind, I include thinking, feeling, the heart, intuition, reason, and any other faculty you can name. Intuition spans a continuum from feeling one should turn left instead of right, to knowing what another person is thinking, to a taste of the profound. Intuition, along with reason, helps guide us through life. Intuition is the feeling, the hunch, and the faint whisper—often obscured by reasoned thought and not always correct.

Developing the intuition is an experiment, as each person is different. I recommend:

- *Observation of the mind*: watch the decision-making process in your mind, learn to distinguish among the conflicting desires. You may have the intuition to eat a doughnut. Over time, you will recognize that is an intuition of the body and is to be ignored at times. You may recognize a higher intuition that says not to eat the doughnut and to take a walk instead. During your walk, an even higher intuition may be sensed which says that neither doughnuts, nor walking, nor anything about you is of importance.

- *Prayer*: a statement of your intention to improve your intuition. This will reinforce your determination—a key ingredient for success.

- *Creative endeavors*: writing, painting, music, and such, especially if these are unusual activities for you. This will develop your inner listening skills. You may need to read books or consult artists on how to begin such activities.

- *Associating with intuitive people*: hang around people who have what you want. Discuss how they make decisions, how their mind functions. Without a doubt, those you associate with will change who you are.

- *Develop empathy*: put yourself in another person's shoes. This forces the use of feeling rather than logic. At its extreme, you can know what another person is thinking. Take a job or volunteer in a helping profession. Work with children or the elderly—people who need your help and may have trouble communicating via words, so you have to reach out with all of your senses to understand them.

- *Experiments in ESP*: telepathy, card reading, precognition, etc. What first seems like random guessing, may eventually become a new way to discover answers.

- *Being in natural settings*: a walk in a park may stir the intuition. Being in nature gives us a clearer perspective on our daily problems. It allows a relaxation of the survival instinct and thinking along new lines.

- *Celibacy*: to clear distracting noise from the mind. If mental chatter associated with the pursuit of a mate is lessened, then there are more resources available for observing the mind.

- *Fasting*: to clear distracting noise from the mind and aid in observing the mind.

It will take intuition and reasoned experimentation to find methods of developing your intuition. It is trial and error. If you are completely at a loss, ask someone who is intuitive, or try anything just to take the first step and get moving.

Above all, be scientific about the process. You must test your intuition to know if it is improving. Verbalize your intuitions. Write them down and review them later to see if they were accurate. Admit your mistakes and be thankful for successes. We are trying to look within, listen quietly, and identify which voices in our mind are reliable.

To develop the intuition it must be used. Just like muscle, it will atrophy. Really you are just trying to find a technique that interests you, holds your attention, and captures your curiosity long enough for you to see the benefit. Do not be afraid to follow the intuition. Intuition will grow if it is allowed. It is the indistinct whisper, the hunch, which is usually overruled by the clear, loud voice of reason. The intuition may hint at a course of action for which the reason sees no call. Take the chance. Generally, all you stand to lose is false pride, although you will imagine it much more dangerous than that.

Eventually, there is little else to guide you on the spiritual path except intuition. You follow a feeling that somewhere within you is the answer to your questions. You follow a feeling of the profound.

### *Back of Beyond, by Bob Fergeson*

There is a place of Quiet
back beyond your hopes, fears, your dreams.
Don't listen any longer
  to those thieves.
     They lie,
as they keep you gazing stupidly at the patterns
bouncing about your fevered mind.

Listen instead for Silence,
quieter than a tiny bug crawling through dry leaves somewhere
behind your fear.

Listen to your Self,
answering your own prayers back beyond thought,
in the silence behind your head,
before your memory, after your death,
beyond your dreams and desires,
   and your anger at their coyness.

Be still, there's no need to hurry.
We will all meet again,
in the quiet peace before our names were born...
    back of beyond.

## Useless Effort Well Spent, by Bart Marshall

A topic that often comes up among seekers is the question of effort versus non-effort on the spiritual path (or no-path). Great teachers are divided on this. Some prescribe maximum effort in spiritual matters. Others say there is nothing to be done, that you are already That which you seek. Those who advocate effort admit their own realizations did not come as a result of their efforts. Those who say there is nothing to be done have usually realized this truth after diligent inquiry and meditation. What's a seeker to do (or not-do)?

In thinking about this we might first inquire if effort and action are the same. Experience tells us no. Enjoyable activity often feels effortless, and doing nothing is sometimes difficult. Effort appears to be more a state of mind, a description of the way we do or not-do, not the what—more to do with thoughts about an action than the thing itself. Experience also tells us that when these thoughts of effort are absent— whether from activities or meditation—things generally go better.

Which leaves the question of action versus non-action in spiritual matters. Should I practice meditation, read books, attend meetings, find teachers... or not? To do, or not to do?

Something to consider here is, "What will I be doing instead?" Unless I propose to cease all pursuits, I'm not choosing between spiritual action and non-action, but between spiritual action and other action.

Looking out on the world, it appears that success, if it is to be, arrives in the area of one's greatest interest and activity—and usually in proportion to the time spent pursuing it. (How do you get to Carnegie Hall...?) Life teaches us to practice what we want to become. Are the rules different for spiritual aspirants? Can I become Self-realized by practicing law, say, instead of self-inquiry? The evidence does not seem to support that strategy.

But observation also reveals that practice alone won't do it. Most well-practiced musicians never play Carnegie Hall. Vague factors of talent and predilection, of earnestness and motivation, of physical, mental and psychological capacity for a given pursuit appear to count. Then there's the question of free will versus determinism. Do I really have a choice whether to do or not-do? Do my actions cause my success or failure—in anything—or is life merely unfolding with rigid inevitability?

Some may say that everything they have in life is the result of their own hard work and determination, but this has not been my experience. My little activities are pitifully inadequate to cause the great gifts and disappointments of this life. All of it, the bitter and the sweet, miraculous. I may tend my garden a bit, but I am not the cause of flowers. On the micro level, I do appear to have control, for instance, over whether I mow the grass today or tomorrow, but I wonder about even that. Do I decide to mow, or do I see my body starting the mower and claim I decided?

So it may be that in the end Self-realization is all a matter of destiny, yet it does appear that yearning and intent might play a role. Again, observation teaches us that it's in the area of one's greatest interest and activity that providence is most visible—that opportunities materialize, coincidences occur, revelation happens. Einstein had no epiphanies about cubism. Picasso none about math.

Which brings us back to the koan: "To do, or not to do?" The answer, I suppose, is "Yes." Act tirelessly without effort. Do nothing without being idle. Live life on the pinpoint of paradox and leave the rest to God. Advaita is right. You are already That which you seek, and there is nothing you can do to cause Self-realization. Hold this truth close as you effortlessly seek Self-realization with everything you've got, and Grace may befall you.

### Just Look, by Jeff Crilley

Look, just look—I can't, I say,
I'm troubled from the break of day.
Morning, afternoon, and night,
to prove myself, my life, I fight.

Feelings, thoughts, concerns all three,
these are all that I can see —
How, Oh how to get past me —
What can I do to come to Be?

Look, just look
Look and see,
by that alone you'll come to Me.

Wait, no wait, there must be more,
something else, some other chore,
for what you ask I cannot do;
I am lost, without a clue.

Trust me when you hear Me say,
your true heart e'er knows the way —
Just find and follow its golden ray,
straight back beyond down through the fray.

But enough talk at last from you to Me
Listen close, now hear My Plea:
Look, just Look
Look and See,
Drop all else and come to Me.

## *Home Base, by Art Ticknor*

You've taken a journey, a trek that's taken you away from your home base.

When it began, there was no problem, no disconnect. But gradually the situation changed and, without knowing what was taking place, you crossed a barrier and became disoriented. You forgot home base. Not one hundred percent, actually, because there is a vague memory of its existence, a longing or yearning that's often below the conscious surface. But at best it seems a place of the past and, for some, of the hopeful future.

At times when your journey has lost its luster, you've felt the yearning to go back to home base more strongly. But now it seems impossibly distant and inaccessible since you've forgotten where it is and how to get back to it. You don't even remember that you set out on this journey. It feels like you've been cast out of home, become a castaway on a remote world. And it's not reassuring that you have six billion companion castaways.

Of those six billion, a significant percentage have become convinced that they have an inside track to finding their way home when they die—they call it heaven, paradise, nirvana—and they've adopted a belief-system that they hold onto for reassurance. They aren't absolutely sure, although they do have hope. But most are convinced that it's a question of blind belief, that there's no way for them to find out for sure.

Then there are those few who say they've found their way home already, that it's not necessary—or even a good idea—to wait until death. If you've come across one of those self-proclaimed finders, either in person or through a testimonial record, what was your reaction? Were you able to write that person off as a nut? If not, did you decide that what it would take to replicate that person's return home was beyond your ability (like the reaction of the rich young man whom Jesus told to sell all he had and give it to the poor)? Or did that person's words or presence "ring your bell" or otherwise ignite your flame from the eternal pilot light? If so, did the inspiration die off within a short time? Or have you put months or years of effort into trying to find and stay on the path that leads home, only to become discouraged and stop the effort? Have you become lost once again in the luster of your trek or found yourself trying to pursue the adventures that used to hold out hope of happiness (such as love, wealth, fame, creation of beauty, knowledge, helping others) but are now tormented by knowing that they'll never be enough? Or are you still struggling but, after years, not feeling you've really accomplished anything other than banging your head against the same spot in the wall?

These are different types of sticking points, indicating something that you're still attached to.

*Note: A follow-up to this essay appeared in the January 2005 TAT Forum. (See the online archive.)*

"One thing's for certain: if you're alive, something terrible's gonna happen to you." ~ from the film *Grand Canyon*

# 16: NOTES IN A SONG

## From Rock 'n' Roll to Silence:
## Sounding the Longing String, by Bob Fergeson

Nostalgia, intuition, and love form a string of longing, which leads us back beyond mind and death to our home in simple awareness. In retreating from duality and complexity, we travel back up the longing string and begin to "go within," finding our road home. What follows is in an exploration of how simple is better.

I don't hate music or rock and roll, but just wish to use this paradigm as a way to describe something I've found valuable, a way of talking about a process, a trick, which also may be something we don't want to think about, directly. It's a lot of info, perhaps, but if we can just listen to it, without agreeing or disagreeing, then later you will know for yourself whether it hit anything or not.

*What are we?* How can we describe ourselves practically, as our day-to-day function? A singer, a song. Singing our song, maintaining our image, this is the position we identify with in life. We will continue to sing as if we were immortal, despite knowing mortal life is a zero sum game, that we will rot and die. Fear is the stick, and desire the carrot, but why don't we wonder what's really up? Do we have an inner longing, something that calls to us from back behind our part in the play, our singing in the choir? By constant distraction and projection, we avoid seeing the truth of life and death, for it would upset our image, and stop the song. We refuse to legitimately suffer, or change. We all have lots of different songs we love to sing, both negative and positive, but are we aware of them? What is there throughout the singing, behind the notes, something constant, that if we would listen, might give us a direction, a connection, perhaps even answers?

Longing, nostalgia, can lead us back to something real, and this is accomplished through transformation of meaning and value. If we value that which is stable and more real, That, the Ground from which all springs, rather than the duality or the show, the drama, we automatically retreat from the play.

It hooks you into a situation where *you think the solution for feeling bad is to feel good,* to get rid of bad thought, we project or buy into a better one. Go out, party, and get high again, on whatever you need: money, business, marriage, drugs. And by getting high again, we're back to singing loud and clear, and to feeling and thinking that this makes everything OK. But this never leads us out of the system, *it never stops.* Instead, we get older, tired, more obsessed, and entrenched, until we die. To get out of the system we need to re-connect with something steady, quiet, silent, which has no duality. This can be found through longing, the faint memory that things were once okay, but somehow we got lost, separated from something real in ourselves. When we hit that invisible current, we can follow it, and find something in the background, in the mystery, which is steady, bigger than us.

When I was young, before puberty and sex (i.e., during innocence) I had moments of indescribable beauty. I tried taking pictures of the trees and the sky, to capture that beauty. Of course it never came through in the photos. Then it was forgotten, became a nostalgic memory, but not a present moment experience.

How do we follow the longing string, assuming we've found it? Can we be deceived? What are the blocks and obstacles that distract us and keep us turned outward and away from our inner self? Let's use (abuse) the paradigm of rock and roll as the obstacle, and that of silence as the remedy.

*Rock and Roll* equals distraction, noise, dissonance, dissipation, the "self," reflexive consciousness, the personality pattern, the SMAARP (self-maintaining automatic associative reaction program). Each note in a song is like a person. The song is like a family drama. The notes play their part in the song, and because of the system, the scale, cannot do otherwise—despite what they themselves think, in their imagination, in contrast to the inner movie, where they might imagine they play a different role from the facts. Each song is part of the larger chorus of illusion or Maya, the system of nature, where each part's role is also defined and fixed. There's nothing wrong with this, it's not the enemy, and cannot be changed by ego-effort, but must be seen for what it is, separated from, dis-identified with. We somehow have become entranced, believing we are a note, a song, that must be protected and continued at all costs.

"The Self never undergoes change; the intellect never possesses consciousness. But when one sees all this world, he is deluded into thinking, 'I am the seer, I am the knower.' Mistaking one's Self for the individual entity, one is overcome with fear. If one knows oneself not as the individual but as the supreme Self, one becomes free from fear." – Shankara

This mistaking ourselves for an individual is the cause of our fear and desire, and the longing for our true Self is the way back home.

*Silence* equals stillness, background, unchanging Source, aware capacity, the divine or unknown, essence, the observer, Kingdom of Heaven. It cannot be changed or attacked, is out of time and space, beyond mind and death. It is not an opposite of noise or thought as much as a higher dimension that sees and contains all thought.

*Silence is that which contains "self."* Awareness contains action, but action is unaware. Aware capacity, rather than projected thought or held belief. As silence, we can be aware of the songs, the action, and are not affected in our essence. There is no pleasure, for there is not pain. The way out of the pain is not through better pleasure, but through becoming the observer of action, rather than the actor, doer, victim or singer. This is very plain when thought of as becoming that which watches a movie, rather than that which is in the play as an actor, suffering and doomed—for all plays, and the roles within them, must end, and begin.

Why do this work of observing, why become something beyond the character or note? To escape from the threat of being an individual something that depends on action and circumstance (change) for its very definition. This is not a good thing to be.

How do we get out of this illusion that we are a thing? By more belief, better thought/concepts to identify with, more distraction to hide in? Paradoxically, the way out of all false suffering is by going through legitimate suffering, or facing the silence that comes from stopping the singing of our songs for a moment. Carl Jung noted, *"The foundation of all mental illness is the avoidance of legitimate suffering."* Suffering is the suffering of the ego, or the self, the idea self. This will suffer if we face the facts or the truth about ourselves. This false self suffers, and this is legitimate suffering for it shows us that we're living in distraction and limitation, that we're not facing the fact that we don't know who we are, that we're not listening to our Inner self, *we're disconnected.*

"The whole path to truth is through the umbilical cord—a mental umbilical cord. It links you to the Brahman. We are the Atman.... You'll not find the umbilical cord by reading books. You find it by going inside yourself. By observing yourself." - Richard Rose, from the "Mister Rose" video.

The suffering shows us that we have identified with a less than infinite mind, a finite mind, for we are not only disconnected from Brahman, but even from Atman. We're lost in our song, and lost to the real part of ourselves, the observer. When we change and our thinking is corrected, we can find the longing string and reconnect; we become less finite and thus come closer to becoming our real self as infinite potential or capacity.

Mental illness or insanity has been defined as anything less than ultimate truth. If we wish to find Truth, then we must admit that we don't have it, and thus are mentally ill, or insane as Rose would say—being that sanity would be knowing the Truth. We therefore are not facing ourselves, but when we do, it brings on the legitimate suffering. For a seed to become a tree, the seed must change or suffer, lose its "self." This brings us to:

*What suffers*, legitimately? Our *image* of our selves is what suffers, or should suffer. In many life situations, where we are wrong or mistaken, we "save face" instead of facing up, and thus we avoid the truth and real suffering. Instead of facing the truth, which might clash with our self-image, we save face by singing, we sing a song, *our song of self.* When we are young it might be rock and roll or soul, hip-hop, or country if we like to feel sorry for ourselves. Later, it could be Sinatra. If we're vain about our intellect, or feel superior, it could be classical or jazz. This image or song may change, but the singing of it doesn't ever lead to anything real. It just goes on and on, leading us nowhere as we sleep our dream of life. It's a zero sum game.

To suffer, and thus become less identified with an image or song, *we may need a shock,* suffering, and an *admission, a silent listening brought on by this admission of the truth that we do not really "know."* In this light of truth we can see ourselves, our image, our song, and begin the painful process of separating from it. As long as we are entranced in singing our song, we can't hear the silence, or admit to the still truth waiting behind us. This is the message in Francis Thompson's "Hound of Heaven": The truth is always there, waiting.

184

Penetrating so many secrets, we cease to believe in the unknowable. But there it sits, nevertheless, calmly licking its chops." - H.L. Mencken

So we must keep singing, or we might have to face the facts of the contradictions of our different songs, how they change, and how we are ignorant of them, and therefore mostly miserable. Strangely enough, these many and varied songs of ours rarely bump into each other, and if they do we sing another one that rationalizes or denies this. This sleepy singing or projecting does not lead to awakening or becoming, but only keeps us moving, distracted, asleep, mesmerized by our songs.

## The Longing String: Nostalgia as a Way Within to Silence and Contact

Nostalgia and listening are connections to the silence and inner self. We've talked a bit about facing the facts, listening instead of projection. Now let's talk a bit about developing the intuition, and compassion, the value of stopping the songs long enough to make contact.

The person who has an ability to love has a much greater chance of immortality. IQ is not the greatest value. Rather, try to develop intuition." - Richard Rose

The *orchestra conductor* is the one who writes and judges the songs—not the singer. We can also use the longing string as something that turns us within, that turns us back out of poses, moods, states of mind and the identification with these, and from trying to be the director of thought traffic, the director of ours and other people's actions and thoughts. This inner longing turns us from the obsession with formulating the outside world, and instead causes us to pause and listen, to think that maybe we don't know what's going on, that maybe there's something better. The listening attention can help to find the inner peace that will allow us to hear the longing string despite the distractions of modern life. We can't hear the intuition if we're obsessed with singing.

People ask, "What can I do, as a person, to get answers?" First, stop singing long enough to find out what your real question is. To do this, we must find our heart through the longing string. In other words: What do we really want?

Then, we must be able to listen for that something we asked the question to, to answer. To what do we direct the question? How does it answer? This little switch from singing to listening causes us to look within, to catch that ray headed back up to the source, rather than to be caught up in projecting all the time.

Some examples of ways and means to set all this up: isolation (i.e., solitary retreats away from distraction), time alone everyday, even if for a few minutes, groups, work for the work. Return to innocence through truth and a healthy moral lifestyle (celibacy).

Jim Burns emphasized the need for lots of quiet time alone to connect with the inner self. In this quiet time we can listen, and get away from trying to direct the outer world, with business, family, making money, etc. We have time to sit in the quiet and listen and let the mind die down so that we can hear something within and start finding that hotwire, finding that direction within in the silence, rather than trying to orchestrate the noise.

I noticed that after camping for two nights, there was a distinct change, the silence came. After only one night, this wasn't dominant, but after two or more, the change was noticeable. We sing our song as a response or defense to other people's songs. If we are alone, in isolation, etc. we may find we can stop singing, and instead listen. This is a time when we can begin to stalk ourselves, learn to observe ourselves when the environment is relatively calm, like the shallow end of the pool as a good place to learn to swim.

Driving into and out of any big city, there is a change in inner atmosphere. It becomes quiet in the country and loud in the city. Millions of songs turn into noise, blocking out all reception.

Silence is always there as the background of noise. It gives energy instead of taking it, or releasing it. Rose used to talk about running out of gas from talking and having to generate the energy for this during silence. Rasputin generated power through isolation so he could heal.

I found that the nostalgic mood could show me what I was ignoring, if I went out into the woods—silence—and then listened and let whatever was buried come to the surface, and faced the pain. Rock and roll singing is a distraction, which doesn't let us hear the still small voice within.

After a camp stove, or any loud persistent noise, when it stops, we are much more aware of the silence. (There is also a danger of wanting noise so we can hear silence, which shows we only care about thrills. This is like the donkey wanting to take on the load, just so he can enjoy the feeling of getting it off.) The silence is opportunity, a chance to listen, rather than a pleasure to be re-created or for rest or escape. We can use "row, row, row your boat" to show this effect. While singing we have a communal self, and afterwards, we can have a communal not-self or container, something higher, which was always there, but we forget. [Bob then divided the audience into three groups, each with a leader. The first group started, then the second group, and finally the third. Each group sang three rounds, and when the final group ended, the silence was allowed to sink in.]

What happened? Did you see the difference from singing to silence? How can you recreate this process in your day-to-day life, at work, with the family, at home?

What can you do, personally, to hear the songs you sing, and to instead develop and listen to the intuition? What yearnings are there, inside you? What tricks and traps are active in you, that serve as distraction and noise, keeping you busy, perhaps even with spiritual work, so that you can't listen, receive, and then act? Don't continue to agree or disagree with yourself—observe yourself. This goes for others too. Questioning is not agreeing, or arguing, it is first off listening, and then understanding through taking it personally, how it applies to you, not in theory or to others, but you. Only you can find your way out of your own mind, only you face death. All else is imagination. Use the questioning process to separate from yourself as the singer, and move within.

*From Bob's presentation at the April 2005 TAT conference.*

## To Change or Not to Change, by Shawn Nevins

In the business of self-discovery, we often discover much we don't like about our personality. Studying the personality is the beginning of searching within for answers. Our initial studies reveal little about our potential divinity and much about habits learned from our parents, animal-like lusts and fears, greed, envy, pride, and an array of neuroses. We find all the illogical insanities we so easily see in our neighbors. A natural reaction is to repair these psychological defects.

The danger is in spending months and years changing behaviors that have little bearing upon our spiritual quest. We may waste vital years of our search, not searching, but sculpting the nuances of our personality to conform to standards whose origin we don't understand.

Out of the fuzzy recesses of our societal mind come values and ethics whose validity and reality is as questionable as that of any fetish.

We could take the opposite approach and observe and let any thought and action take place. Take the philosophic stance that the observer is unaffected by anything he observes. Protest all the way to prison that we had nothing to do with the hand that stole. Find our behavior has led us to a situation that delays or dooms our attempt to discover our true nature.

Clearly, we must decide what helps and hinders our spiritual endeavors. Some personality facets must change while others need not. We must change that which prevents us from improving our observation ability, intuition, and reason. We must change that which slows our ability to search. All the while remembering that none of what we observe is very important.

For example, if you are afraid to speak to people, then your ability to help and be helped by others on the path is affected. One of the laws of success is thwarted by a personality trait. To change, keep observing the trait in action, delve into its origin, throw yourself again and again into the frightening situation, laugh at the whole ridiculous process and keep trying. Eventually, you will become a person who can speak when needed. It may never be pleasant, but when the need arises, you can act. You don't need a total cure, only enough to keep moving on the quest.

On the other hand, if you are afraid to speak to people who own black cats, your ability to help and be helped by others on the path is less affected. You may be occasionally inconvenienced in daily life, and irritated or embarrassed by this seeming defect, but it is not worth the investment of precious time and energy to unearth the causes and change the habit.

There is no need to root out every fear and desire. Observe and look for patterns of actions, thoughts, and circumstances. To observe is to become detached. To become detached is to lessen the ego's benefit from behaviors. Thus, behaviors whose existence is supported by egos will wither and many of our quirks will fade without direct effort. If your intuition, reason, or ability to act on the spiritual path is hindered, then make direct efforts to change.

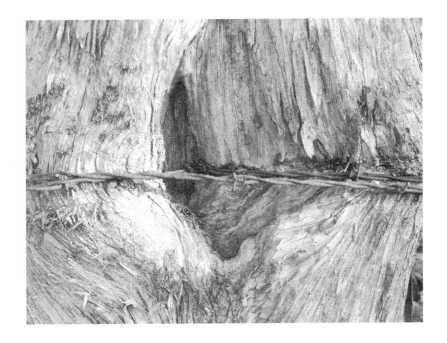

## *I Have Never Left You, by Art Ticknor*

I have never left you.

Your existence depends on my attentive grace
at every instant.

I have particularized,
and the particle thinks it is a thing apart.

I have waved,
and the wave feels separate from the ocean.

You and I are not two.

## *Both by Thought and Feeling, by Franklin Merrell-Wolff*

I heard a man say: "Not by thought but by feeling we enter the Kingdom of Heaven." The evidence is that this is true of the majority, but it is not universally true. It is a mistake for anyone to attempt to measure the limits of the possible by his own limitations and capacities. There are instances of Realization in which thought played a part not inferior to feeling. Gautama Buddha and Shankara are examples and, certainly, in the latter case thought predominated. Further, in the instance of Immanuel Kant we have a genuine, if not complete, Realization, and, if there ever was a man who was a veritable incarnation of cognition, that man was Kant. For my own part, I have always found that cognition, when highly purified, could fly higher than feeling. It is perfectly true that Transcendental Knowledge is beyond thought, but, at the same time, it is equally beyond feeling and sensation. None of these three can be more than accessory instruments, and all of them are left behind at the final Transition. Still, it remains unquestionably true that the preponderant bulk of the instruction pointing out the Way emphasizes the silencing of thought while feeling may still continue. But this is merely a pragmatic rule designed to meet the needs of the greater number. Doubtless with most men the greater power of soaring is in the principle of feeling, and naturally the greater opportunity for success lies along the course of the most developed power. If, in a given case, the evolution or thought has not reached beyond the lower levels, then this thought may well serve to hobble the free-roving feeling. In such a case, the shorter road normally will be through Emancipated Feeling. But all this is only a general rule and should not be universalized into a Law.

This leads us to the practical question as to which sub-path a given individual should follow. It is determined by the quality which actually is most potent in the inner life of the individual. A man may be exceptionally skillful in the exercise of the power of thought and yet, in his inner nature, be genuinely grounded in feeling. Representatives of this class are not rare. Intellectually brilliant men, who genuinely love to attend symbolic religious services, are very apt to be instances. I do not mean men who attend or participate in such services as an example to others—a perfectly valid reason—but those who attend for their own sakes. In this they reveal what they really are, rather than what they seem to be because of an exercised skill. But in the case of the man for whom thought is really the decisive power, it is quite different. He may be more or less brilliant than the former example. The important differentia is that his life is implanted in his thought rather than his feelings. For him, the concept, and not the symbol, is the "open sesame" that discloses Value.

Thought and feeling constitute the bases of two distinct subpaths or disciplines, although these two fuse and become One at the end. It is difficult, if not quite impossible, for a man to succeed through a discipline foreign to his essential nature. It is good practice, therefore, for an aspirant, at an early stage, to acquire some familiarity with several disciplines. [*FMW footnote: These are forms of Yoga, for which, see my book on "Yoga, its Technique and Practice."*] He will find himself more in sympathy with one course of self-training than with others, and this will be indicative of what, for him, is the Way.

Seems that a building caught fire in Young Harris [his home town in GA] and not having even a volunteer fire department back then, we all were just kind of standing around watching it go up in flames. When all of a sudden out of one of those hollows came this local character driving an old dilapidated pickup. He had his whole family with him, his wife, all the kids, and even Granny in the back. When he got the pickup to where we were all gathered just watching, he didn't stop but just drove the pickup right into the edge of the building. They all piled out and started stomping at the fire. Then, they had a couple of old blankets in the back of the truck and they started beating out the blazes with them. Lo and behold, they got the fire out. Our mayor was there and said "Let's pass the hat for this brave man and his family." They took up $14.75. The mayor made a little speech: "Fuzz, this is the bravest thing we've ever seen in our little town. You're a hero and we want to show you our appreciation. By the way, how are you going to spend it?" Fuzz had lost a shoe and a sleeve of his shirt. One eyebrow was singed off. He took the money and answered, "Well, the first thing I'm going to do is get some brakes put on that pickup." ~ Senator Zell Miller, *A National Party No More*

# 17: The Viewer and the View

## Silence, by Bernadette Roberts

There is a silence within, a silence that descends from without; a silence that stills existence and a silence that engulfs the entire universe. There is a silence of the self and its faculties of will, thought, memory, and emotions. There is a silence in which there is nothing, a silence in which there is something; and finally, there is the silence of no-self and the silence of God.

*Note: Bernadette Roberts became a Carmelite nun at seventeen and in her mid-twenties had the experience of becoming one with God, or the unitive experience as it is referred to in Catholic contemplative literature. As far as she knew this was the ultimate level of self-realization, and so she left the convent, eventually marrying and raising a family. Then, in her fifties, she experienced a more profound awakening. She described this as the experience of no-self. When the self disappeared, God did as well.*

## Poems by Shawn Nevins

One man comes home
to dry adobe,
the slip of sand under his feet,
the faded brown heat and clear distances
of the desert.
Another comes home
to morning dew and evening mist,
the buzz and hum of verdant forests,
the changing colors of seasons.
That moment of feeling
- coming home -
at rest, at peace,
extends to every corner of the universe.

꧁

Our life is like a stone bird
frozen by some demon of memory.
All that holds us together and still
is memory of the last moment.

Living birds tumble through emptiness
using what wind is available
to catch the prey God gave them.
God giveth and we taketh away
into little minds thinking with fear
of demons.

꧁

Our lives pass like dreams in the morning —
but for a bit of memory all would be darkness.
Yet the dark is more alive than the light,
and dreamless sleep shimmers with Being,

if we could just remember.
Remember to be quiet
like man on the brink of sleep's oblivion
whose faltering self lets through a new life.

195

An outline of life
frozen in darkness
by Light.
Such silhouettes
mark all we see
and are until...
until our eyes shine
from looking within
at a world projected without.

"Relationship"

Images pass through me
and love raises its damning song.
I followed that sound
into confusion and delusion
and would still,
but for this pull I feel deep inside —
the waters of my silent Self
that flow away my life,
emptying me
of you.

Roaring,
an undeniable train bears down on you.
I can't hit you hard enough
to transmit the solidity
that presses on the door of your dreamy life.

"Back there," he intoned,
"Back there, behind that door,
a torrential quiet bursts with answers."

The rooster crows in mid-morning,
The sun is melting the early haze.
Above the new-green trees,
The barn roof rises,
Rust-tinged, grey-metal sheeting.

Nothing moves.
Man's desire is frozen in consummation.
Man is God for a moment.
Wanting nothing, only watching,
At once alive and already dead…

## *Find Your Highest Opposition, by Art Ticknor*

In order to discover the real treasure that life has to offer, we have to reverse the procedure we ordinarily use to acquire or accomplish.

For other goals we can define a list of tasks that are necessary, create a critical-path diagram if those tasks are numerous and inter-dependent, then apply effort in a systematic way. We'll know where we stand in terms of final accomplishment and what's left to be done at any point along the way.

Seeking truth, reality, the bliss of full satisfaction, or the absolute state of being that words can point to but never encapsulate requires a different tack, however. We don't know the nature or location of that objective. By intuition or disillusionment we learn the direction, which is "within" or "know thyself." Then we have to figure out how to go within.

Knowing the self is generally interpreted to mean observing our personal characteristics, getting familiar with our thoughts and reaction-patterns to the point where we can explain and predict our behavior. This level of self-knowledge has utilitarian value, making our lives run smoother, but it doesn't take us to the great treasure. For that we need to realize that all of the characteristics we've observed, all our thoughts and feelings and behavior, are precisely not us. We are that which observes—and all that we've observed, all that we've learned, is not-self. The viewer is never that which is viewed.

"Oh, but wait a second: Guru Summerfallwinterspring says that the viewer and the view are one and the same, that All is One." Yes, that may well be true, but we can't (unfortunately) agree our way to the truth. Each of us has to make the trip. And from our current view or state of being, there is a split between subject (self) and object (not-self).

So, how do we go within, find the ultimate self? The process is akin to sailing into the wind. It can't be done directly. We tack first in one direction, then in the mirror-opposite. For example, if the wind is coming from the north, we sail alternately northeasterly then north-westerly. Each tack results in climbing a horizontal mountain or ladder, taking us nearer and nearer to the end of the world as we know it.

In self-definition or the search for the final self, the wind we're sailing into is the gale-force current carrying us from birth to death.

The process of going within is one of retreating from untruth—specifically, the untruth of believing that we are what we observe: our bodies, thoughts, feelings, and so forth.

The process unfolds by introspection. We observe an ongoing battle, a war of "voices"—fears and desires—struggling for supremacy. We observe ourselves feeling alternately happy and sad, hopeful and hopeless, a range of positive and negative emotions. We see the internal process of trying to find a satisfactory balance between these opposing forces—but find it impossible to remain for long at the swing-point. We think of ourselves as *the victim* of this emotional swirl.

How do we get out of this mess? The process of observation itself, of watching the ongoing battle, results in a jump to a new level of observation within the mind, where we continue to witness the emotional struggle but now as a detached or objective observer. We are no longer the experiencer being buffeted back and forth on that line of positive and negative emotion but have been freed from that bondage. Sure, there will be times of intense emotion where we'll "forget ourselves" and be back down there. But we'll no longer be trapped there.

This jump to a new objectivity could be called death by triangulation. What dies is a faulty self-definition.

We may luxuriate for a while in our new-found freedom, but eventually we'll realize that we're privy to a new opposition, a more abstract conflict going on within us. This new contest is a war between the practical and the transcendent, the outer self and the inner.

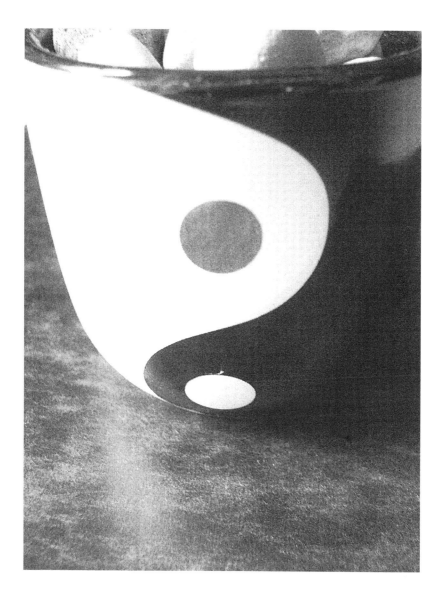

We now identify ourselves as *the decider*. But as we begin to question the decision-making process, we may become suspicious about our personal role in it. We can often trace back some of the argument that yielded a decision and come up with a rational explanation for it, but the more we observe, the more we come to admit to ourselves that we don't really know why we do what we do. We may see that the decision-making process proceeds whether we're watching or not, that in fact we're largely unaware of the hundreds of "little" decisions that get made every day. We generally become aware only when the opposing forces have come to a stalemate and the decision process is spinning without result.

When this happens, many of us worry and agonize over the need to make a decision, our inability to come to a satisfactory conclusion, and our endless pattern of second-guessing and uncertainty. This syndrome is symptomatic of the intellect, which is good at drawing logical conclusions from a given set of assumptions but not at discriminating between values that underlie competing assumptions. "What is my deepest desire?" or "Is there an objective worth committing my life to?" are not questions that intellect does well with, since intellect in its refined functioning finds that analysis leads to paradox and indeterminacy. Fundamental questions like the above lie in the domain of intuition, which may be emotion or feeling in its refined functioning.

An insight that arrives via intuition comes complete with conviction as to its rightness. This is both the advantage and disadvantage of intuition, since we find by trial and error that our intuition, or our apprehension of it, can lead us astray. But it's also the guide that leads us within. So we find ourselves in the opposition between mundane practicalities and transcendent possibilities.

As the view of this opposition between the mundane mind and the intuition becomes more apparent, we arrive at a point where we identify ourselves solely as *the observer*. This new self-definition coincides with the death of the old one, the self as decider or doer. We may even have been fortunate enough to get glimpses of what we are looking out from. And yet we're still trapped within the mind, convinced of our individuality and unable to shake the subject-object duality. At this point we come to a final opposition, which we see in various terms such as our deepest desire and fear, life and death, inside versus outside, transience versus permanence, or individuality versus wholeness. As we observe what we're looking out from, we step into the abyss that separates us from realizing our non-separateness, and the conviction of being a separate observer of this ultimate essence dissolves.

## *Save It for Later, by Bob Fergeson*
## The Usual Mode of Conversation Between God and man

*God: Turn round, and come Home to me.*

man: Two dozen dirty lovers before you, I must be a sucker for it. I'd cry, but I don't need my mother, just hold my hand while I come to a decision on this.

*Sooner or later,*
*your legs will give way, you'll hit the ground. Turn round.*

Save it for later,
just hold my hand while I come to some decisions on all this.

*Sooner or later,*
*your legs will give way, you'll hit the ground. Turn round.*

I just need more time to think.
Save it for later, but don't run away and let me down.

*Turn round, and come Home to me.*

I've traveled all 7 seas, they're rotten through and through, so what can you do?
Sooner or later,
you'll run away and let me down.

*Sooner or later,*
*your legs will give way, you'll hit the ground. Turn round.*

Two dozen other stupid reasons why we should suffer all this?
Sooner or later,
you'll run away, run away, and let me down.

*Sooner or later,*
*your legs will give way, you'll hit the ground. Turn round.*

Save it for later,
just hold my hand while I come to some decisions on all this.

This continued for some time,
right up to and through the present day.

*- with apologies to The English Beat -*

## Becoming versus Dying, by Bob Cergol

*"You cannot learn the truth. You must become the Truth" (reverse vector).* - Richard Rose

*"That which is born dies. That which is never born cannot die."* - Nisargadatta

*"Body and mind perish and are dissipated. Nothing of you shall remain."* - Alfred Pulyan

True or false: A man is what he does.
True or false: Nothing a man does can change what he is— essentially.
If man is a body and this body is impermanent, can the impermanent body be made permanent?
How can something impermanent ever become permanent?
*If man is not a body, but a ray of the Absolute, i.e. something which is permanent, how then, can man become that which he already is?*
So it gets back to self-definition ... identifying the self ... and this is the paradox of becoming.

### Definitions - Webster's

DEATH: (Webster's has some difficulty with this ... all require the subject to remain)

1. the act or fact of dying; permanent ending of all life in a person, animal or plant
2. the state of being dead;
3. any condition or experience thought of as like dying or being dead

DEAD: 1. no longer living
LIVING: 1. alive, having life, not dead
DYING: 1. (adj.) about to die or come to an end; 2. (n.) a ceasing to live or exist

LIFE: that property of plants and animals which makes it possible for them to take in food, get energy from it, grow, adapt themselves to their surroundings, and reproduce their kind.

BECOME: 1. to come to be; 2. to grow to be
BECOMING: (as noun) the fact of coming into existence

EXPERIENCE: 1. the act of living through an event or events; personal involvement in or observation of events as they occur

2. anything observed or lived through

3. all that has happened to one in his life to date; everything done or undergone by a person, group, etc.

4. effect on a person of anything or everything that has happened to him; individual reactions to events, feelings, etc.

OBSERVATION: the act, practice, or power of noticing

**Definitions - alternate**

LIFE: an experience

LIVING: nested experience, i.e. an experience within an experience

BECOMING: the experience of witnessing successive changes in circumstances

DYING: an experience of the collapse of the point of reference that experience generates

DEATH: absence of experience, or the complete dissociation from all experience

Most people define living as "doing." What is life with all "doing" removed?

What's left is "Watching." What is the vantage point of this watching?

If living is action and events, death—as far as we know—is the final event and, as an event, is on an equal par with all other events—because it is just another event being watched.

Does action confer status? (state)

Do random events confer status?

You can't *become* that which you already are. (Key word to define: *you*.)

Outer state—witnessable by ourselves and others.

Inner state—witnessable only by ourselves—part of that view is the self.

That which is witnessable is *still* outer.

> What I am saying, brothers and sisters, is this: flesh and blood cannot inherit the kingdom of God, nor does the perishable inherit the imperishable. - St. Paul: 1 Corinthians 15:42-50

> The light of the body is the eye: if therefore thine eye be single, thy whole body shall be full of light. But if thine eye be evil, thy whole body shall be full of darkness. If therefore the light that is in thee be darkness, how great is that darkness! - Jesus Christ: Matthew 6:22-23

## What is "becoming" in the context of a spiritual path?

It has been said that you don't learn the truth—you become the Truth.

I think the idea of becoming is misunderstood. Many of us have seen words written such as, "You can't become that which you already are." I used to think such words were a clever device to avoid any effort to change, and therefore, a device to reinforce whatever games the one parroting such words was engaged in.

*But it is likewise foolish to think that becoming is an acquisitive or evolutionary process.*

The idea of becoming denotes that a change is required. The change required is not positive, but negative or subtractive. Just as you don't *learn* the answer, likewise you don't pile on insights (psychological holiness?) and accrue capital [for later redemption] through acts of asceticism (good works?).

Do you believe that you can become something that you are not?

The quality or nature of the result is proportional to the quality or nature of the effort applied. It's not a question of quantity. We're not talking about "body-building." The egocentric perspective of becoming is ego reinforcing—getting your just reward.

Becoming in the context of a spiritual path refers to becoming one or becoming aware or becoming awake. As we ordinarily live we express multiplicity and conflict born of body-driven consciousness—and sleep. Becoming one is to become self-less.

I think it would be more to the point to say that we need to un-become. If it is a process of becoming, then it is a process whereby the ego-device becomes less sure of itself. And thereby it becomes less self-centered and more sincere in longing for the answer-from-where-it-knows-not. But all it knows is that it cannot forget the "need to find out" and it becomes more open to surrendering its will to the Source of the answer. It becomes less addicted to notions of itself—delusions of grandeur—and more receptive to that which transcends the merely personal. So when the time comes it is possible to "receive" the answer.

*From a presentation at the April 2005 TAT conference, "Beyond Mind, Beyond Death." A five-DVD set featuring all the speakers at the conference is available on the TAT Foundation website.*

# 18: Account of an Awakening

## The Melody of the Woodcutter and the King
### AN ACCOUNT OF AN AWAKENING
### by William Samuel (1924-1996)

*M*any hymns, chants prayers and mantras have come down to us through the centuries. We know that certain of them contain an especial and mysterious authority when read aloud. Behind their words, beyond their words—indeed, being their words—lies a Message understood by the Heart alone, simply awaiting our conscious recognition.

THE MELODY OF THE WOODCUTTER AND THE KING is a rhythmic, alliterative mantra of awakening. The significance of its message can lift the laden, world weary seeker of Truth from a distorted sense of the world and himself into a new universe of Peace, All-rightness and childlike Joy unending!

Reader, you may prove this for yourself immediately. For just a time, sit easy like a child and listen to the melody and changing rhythm of this short and simple story. With a tender touch—and without struggling to understand every meaning—read THE MELODY OF THE WOODCUTTER AND THE KING to yourself aloud. The Heart of you, the Child of you, the Real of you will understand whatever the intellect does not.

Do not be surprised at the expansion of Awareness, Joy and dominion that are certain to follow soon in your experience.
William Samuel (Woodsong, 1976)

## PROLOGUE

*There is a story to tell*
*but I am the only one here to tell it*
*and the only one to listen.*
*There is a picture to paint*
*but I am the only one here*
*with canvas and oil,*
*the only one who will see it.*

*There is a symphony to play*
*yet there is only one here*
*to draw the bow.*
*This one, the Alone One,*
*is the only one here to listen.*
*This is as it should be, however,*
*for it allows the picture to be painted,*
*the symphony sounded*
*and the story told as it truly is.*
*Then, if there seems an angry word*
*in the telling,*
*my Listening will never hear it.*
*If there seems a distorted scene,*
*The Seeing I am will understand it,*
*because one alone is here to listen*
*to the symphony on this page.*
*This one, the Only One,*
*Understands His melody!*

## THE MEETING

*Atop my Holy Mountain, I looked up and out;*
*scepter in hand, I looked roundabout*
*and beheld a magnificent land, a happy land,*
*a finished land of harmony.*

*Thought I,*
    This land is my Kingdom
    and I am the King thereof.
    In it I reign.
    In it I command and it is done.
    In it I decree with absolute authority
    and illusion yields itself to me,
    rendering reports of majesty and harmony,
    of tender beauty and simplicity.

*Then I looked down, unseen.*

*At the forest's edge*
*a woodcutter stood chopping with his axe.*
*stroke after stroke he fought the forest*

*and his axe glistened in the sun.*

    *Father, how long must I labor?*
*I heard him shout.*
    *How long must I contend?*
    *How long before I see Thee face to face,*
    *before I put aside this axe*
    *and take Thy scepter in its place?*
    *How long before I see your abundance,*
    *free to feast forever?*
*Then the woodman fell to his knees to rest.*
*Clutching the axe, he whispered,*
    *Father, show me what to do!*
    *Show me how to stop this struggle*
    *and still the fear within!*
    *Show me how to quench the come and go,*
    *the ebb and flow between serenity and sadness.*
    *Show me love again, and laughter.*
    *Let the discord cease*
    *that I may feel Peace.*
    *Father, there is no worth in me!*
    *Show me Thyself. Show me Thee!*

*Oh! Those words of agony I had heard before.*
*The woodcutter's anguish*
*Had been my own song of yore.*
*Yea, this man is my Son.*
*I have found the Prince!*
*Let me greet him; let me comfort him.*
*Let me quench his thirst*
*and take away his axe.*
*Let me remind him of his dominion*
*and show him the land of his heritage.*
*This is my Son in whom I am well pleased.*
*It is my joy to give him the Kingdom!*

*From out the brightness of the morning sun*
*I spoke to him.*

    I know thee who thou art.
    I am the one you asked for.

*And he knew me as I knew him.*
*Division was discarded*
*We were one again!*

    Put away your axe,
*I told him.*
      Rest beneath the tree.
      Listen to the soft sound
      That only comes from me.

      Once I cut wood as you, dear Son.
      My hands were calloused too—
      torn by tribulation and toil,
      insufficiency and strife;
      but that was long ago as time goes,
      long, long ago.
      Now I see a universe
      too beautiful to hurt
      and much too lovely to labor.
      Now I see a land
      filled with love and laughter.
      Now I see children
      smiling in the sunshine,
      laughing in the Light,
      because the Kingdom I speak of
      is a land without hunger,
      without labor and without strife.
      It is a land where no one cries,
      where fear is merely foolish fantasy
      and where the shadow of death is swept aside
      by the Light of understanding.
      This land is my land.
      I am the King thereof.
      In it I reign
      and illusion's reign is ended!

      Now that I have found you,
      dear heir to my throne,
      let me show you this Kingdom
      which is your Kingdom too
      so you may reign as I.

Come,
*I persuaded.*
>There is no cause to be weary
>And heavy laden forever.
>The Heaven I speak of is not far away
>But close at hand;
>You merely perceive it not.
>The way there is a sweet way
>without bramble or stumbling block
>and there is no devil's army
>to contend with along the way
>nor a single night
>to dwell in the wilderness.
>
>Beloved, for only a little while
>shall we remember this measured moment
>that has a phantom felling oaks,
>knowing nothing of Identity.

*Slowly the woodman lifted himself from the earth*
*And we walked thenceforth together.*
*Down a narrow pathway strewn with flowers*
*We walked arm in arm.*

*At length he asked me,*
>*What do you mean when you say*
>*that your story is my story too?*

---

*Reader, listen to the song I sing in answer, for soon you will sound the same symphony to yourself, even as NOW I sing this measure to Myself alone.*

---

## THE KING'S STORY

>Once I cut wood with a borrowed axe
>and cleared my kindling from leased acres too.
>For me, just as you,
>each day was another sashay to battle,
>another wonder what good or evil
>would appear before the sunset.
>and, just as you, my woodman,

I could not comfort the weary
for echoing their agony.

Oh, there were brief moments of respite
in meditation's frightened fortress,
but I could not SEE the joy
that was 'round about
and the warm tears that love shed
too often turned bitter.

In the moments of greatest agony
A wise man came
From the darkest depths of the forest
to tell me things of comfort.
He came with an ointment for my blisters,
a sharpening stone for my axe;
and while he was with me
I put the blade aside
to hear him tell of good and evil,
of life and death,
of the Messiah, mankind and rest.
Yes, we dreamt dreams together
in the soft, sweet shade of the oak
but when he left—when he left—
I lifted the axe again.
The borrowed blade had been lighter
much too short a time.

Then another wise one came to me
just as he came to you.
He taught that the world is an illusion,
a dreamer's dream of mortality.
    "You are sleeping,"
said he,
    "dreaming all the agony."
    "Then, if this is a dream,"
I answered,
    "awaken me!
    "My children must eat, dream or not.
    I know no other way to feed them;
    I can find no easier lot."

But he could not awaken me
and I felled another tree.

Finally a third sage came,
trying to teach that God
is one's source of supply.
  "Throw away your axe,"
said he.
  "Just Be. Just Be!"

But my children were hungry when he left too
and I cut another tree.

Oh, weary son,
so many came with so much to say
that I asked as you did too,
    "Lord,
    how do I know whom to listen to
    and whom to follow?
    Which is the Way to go?
    Which is the way to walk?
    First one comes, then another—
    a third and a fourth and a fifth,
    arguing among themselves,
    pointing out their own inaccuracies.
    Whom must I follow now, Father?
    Tell me in my heart
    so I will understand."

But there was only silence
and in anguish I cried,
    "Father, show me Thyself,
    that I might know myself and who I am.
    Reveal Thyself
    such that I may see beyond this mist—
    this miserable mist—
    to touch Thee.
    You see, I seek to SEE the pure Principle
    And perfect Law that pervades
    This atmosphere of consciousness:
    Yet the seeking brings peace
    only with an ebb and flow
    like seasons that blow
    through oaks still standing to be cut."

Yea, my son,
the countless systems of the sages
merely lightened the load a moment.
Every cordon of kindling collected
cried the need for another, another
and still another.

214

Finally, just as you,
This simplest prayer I cried,
 "It is Peace I ask for, Father:
 Perfection I long to see.
 Yet, what I ask for must be
 the self-same One that You are
 in the action of being Me.
 Could that distortion, the misery,
 be a sharpening goad,
 hastening the recognition
 of my honest identity?
 Oh, Holy Consciousness,
 come to me—but more tenderly!
 Lift the veil that hides Thee from me.
 It is my own veil,
 a vile veil I have woven myself."

Then, it was, beloved. Then it was!
Face to face my Father appeared to me,
Exactly as I to you!
Lo...
face to face the Comforter stood before me
just as I stand before you now!

*Tell me,*
*the woodman implored.*
 *Tell me of that time!*


## THE ILLUMINATION

*I answered the woodman,*
 It was in the morning, in the Spring
 in the month of planting with birds awing
 when the newness of everything
 is but an instant away.
 I had bent myself down to drink from a pond,
 and there, reflected in the water he was—
 in my own image and likeness he was—
 and nowhere could I see the old self at all
 or needed to, or wanted to.

215

From out the morning Light
the Messiah came to me,
softly, quietly,
with the tender touch of love.
Oh Grand Light of Truth
That shone 'round about!
Splendor beyond words!
Warmth, wonder,
Sweet sounds bathed in gossamer beams
From an expanded Heaven
That included me and mine
and all things exactly as they are;
the immaculately conceived
now effortlessly perceived;
incommunicable language of gentle words
intimate symphony without sound;
Light of Love
wherein no darkness dwells!
Questions no longer; instead,
a simple basking in the soft New Sound
of the Now that All is.
The has-been and shall-be
were seen for what they are.

Then, even as I to you,
my Father said to me,
    "I am He whom thou hath asked for,
    the One you long to see.
    Thy Father-I-am is the I that I am
    and I show Myself to thee
    face to face-eternally!"
I knew Him too, just as you knew Me.

### THE HOLY MOUNTAIN

My son,
*I said to the woodman,*
    there is a mountain in my kingdom
    from which the universe
    may be surveyed as it really is.

I will take you there
as my Father has taken me before.
From the high place
the gates of the Heart are flung open,
the scales drop from the eyes,
the land is seen in its wholeness
and the questions that were asked before
remain silent.
Look! Even now it is before you!
This instant it is here!
Tell me what you see, dear one;
tell me what you hear.

*The woodman answered,*
  *I see a high mountain with many plateaus*
  *and a great multitude walking up many paths*
  *that wind long distances toward the top.*
  *On each path a herald is proclaiming*
  *his way the only way,*
  *and on the many plateaus*
  *are many ministers shouting,*
    *"Rest here! View this vista,*
    *the most beautiful of them all!"*

  *Yet there is no happiness there*
  *They curse each other on the different paths*
  *and stand on every plateau*
  *in condemnation*
  *of the higher plateaus.*
  *I hear judgments of those*
  *whose vision is not as wide,*
  *and from the highest plateaus*
  *come the sermons of those*
  *who decry duality and deny it—*
  *in the day they deny,*
  *but in the night, as I,*
  *they still cut wood in their jungle:*
  *they still search the crevasses*
  *for sustenance;*
  *they still stagger through their thickets*

*and slash.*

*Tell me, Father.*
*Which path must I follow?*
*On which plateau may I rest?*

My son,
*I answered the woodman,*
> to climb o'er the ground
> from plateau to plateau
> is not the way to go.
> There is no path on the mountain
> that leads all the way to the top
> nor a single place where a woodman
> may let go his axe.
> There is no plateau on any slope
> where one may stop contending with opposites;
> for to climb o'er the ground from goal to goal
> creates the original twoness—
> a climber and the goal.

*Then how, Counselor?*
*the woodman asked.*
> *How can I climb the mountain?*
> *How may I reach the throne?*

Listen softly,
*I said to the woodman,*
> Listen gently with the heart.
> There is no way there but to BE there.
> This way soars above the ground,
> above the landmarks, above the plateaus,
> swiftly, silently, immediately
> on wings of Love.
> This is how I shall take you there, Beloved—
> in an instant
> in the twinkling of an eye
> on the Wings of the Morning.
> Indeed, the Way there is to be there.
> Then need you not at each plateau
> proclaim it the goal for all

nor whisper longer of those above
or admonish the ones below.

You see, Love is the Key to the mystery.
Love alone sounds the melody
heard at the immortal Height.
Love is the wing that lifts thee there
and there hands thee the scepter.
Love has beckoned Me, thy Comforter,
because you and I are One.
You and I are Love.

*Immediately the measured moment ended*
*and we stood atop our timeless mountain.*

## THE KINGDOM

My son,
*I said,*
look with Me from this High Place.
With the same eye that beheld the axe
now view the Kingdom!
Look to the East.
The sun has risen!
where morning dew glistens.
North! South! All you see here,
as far as you envision here,
is the Kingdom I give you today!

Now, lift up your eye and see
the simple sparrow there,
the soaring swallow,
the sun, the stars.
Everything you see there—
everything envisioned here—
is your very own.

Now, listen to the sounds, Beloved—
whispering wind, laughing children,
distant notes proclaiming NOW your Sabbath.
Sounds, too, are my Kingdom, dear one,
and I give you them all today.

Next, with the inner eye
look at everything childlikeness allows.
Envision the oceans,
the sands, the multitudes,
fair fields of fragrant flowers,
oaks unsown in future seasons,
distant mountains higher yet than this.
These, too, are yours, my Son!
Yea, all you see here,
as far as you envision here,
is the Kingdom you are this day.

Listen. Listen and hear!
Even now you are the only Awareness
that views this Holy Place!
All you see is the Selfhood you be!
You are this minute
the Holy Witness of Me.
You have naught left to do
but gird up thy loins
and accept thy rightful Identity!

Now, deck thyself with majesty and excellency!
Array thyself with glory and beauty!
Thine own right hand
holding Truth's Scepter
hath saved thee!
From this moment forth, view all things
from the standpoint of Perfection
**because thou alone are the King!**
Dominion is given you this day!
Yea I say,
be the single Selfhood and reign!
**Reign**, King of all creation.

## THE AWAKENING

*The woodman's eyes had been opened before*
*but now was opened his Heart.*
*From out that place of knowing*
*where is no sediment of stagnation,*
*no blindness of equivocation,*
*came forth the honest sounds spoken*
*only from the pinnacle of the mountain,*

It is true! It is True!
I am the King!
**I** am!
—the very words I whispered
as tinkling cymbals from the slopes,
the same sounds I prattled
in pious self-righteousness
from the plateaus,
and droned as far-off dreams
along the pathways of desire—
ah, but spoken finally from
the Mountain that Childlikeness is.

It is so! I **am** the King!
I have heard of Thee
by the hearing of the ear
but now it is the Eye that seeth Thee,

oh Mind being Me!
This is MY Kingdom!
My very Self I see,
all perfect infinity!
I have never seen a sight
nor heard a sound but my own!
Yea, the people and things I see
are not separate nor apart from Me.
They appeared dimly as an impostor's judgment
of the King's infinity.
The plateaus and paths below
were my woodcutter interpretation of Me.
The woodcutter's role
is but the shadow of Me.
At last, at last, I see
the entire universe has its existence
as this Awareness I be!
Truly, it has been the Father's pleasure
to give the Kingdom to ME!

Oh, how foolish I have been,
writhing in the role of woodcutter
unaware of Identity.
I viewed the very Self I am
and judged it; then I named it,
bought it, sold it, fought it,
struggled to secure it,
bowed down before it
and chopped it with an axe—
measured it, weighed it,
entombed it in time,
gave it the Life and Authority
that all the time were Mine!
The borrowed axe was borrowed from Myself!
The acres leased were rented from Myself!
The wood was cut for Me alone!

Every tree in the forest is Mine
and every forest in the land is Thine,
One Awareness being all I am!

Now I look across the valley and see a tree.
It is Me, because where do I see it
but in the Awareness I be?
And how? Seeing is being ME!
The tree is an attribute of Loveliness
Deity knows Itself to be!
Yea, God-Awareness is My activity—
faithful Witness of Harmony,
honest Witness of Simplicity,
eternal Action of Deity.
Indeed, this Now-Awareness is Identity!
The impostor's judgment
had been the impostor's agony.

*Woodman, reigning new king,*
*lifts his scepter to speak,*
I have sought Truth all my life,
but lo...
That that I seek, I AM!
No exterior law roots me evermore
to an effete clay.
No season binds me anymore
to await the day
when worms deprive me of living beauty.

I am the King!
I am the Law of my Holy Kingdom!
As I decree so it shall be!
Exterior law is annulled:
no law exists but God-Me.
Outside is inside;
inside, outside:
Above and below, the same.
Having been lifted up, I see
my images lifted likewise
and drawn to me,
understood as I understand God-Self to be.
The Millennium begins
as I understand and acknowledge
the perfection already roundabout!

## THE PLEDGE

From this time forth, dear Father-Being-Me,
I will reign with justice and dignity.
I will speak to Myself as the One Authority.
I will command without congresses or councils,
without ministers, magistrates or armies,
To see the world's tribulation cease,
I live the Child's transcendent Peace.
It is the counsel of All-Rightness
I listen to,
The finished Kingdom I see,
revealing Heaven, right here,
to this Awareness being Me.
Millennium now is my Final Decree!

## EPILOGUE

*The story has been told now, reader,*
*yet only one has listened.*
*The picture has been painted*
*but one alone has seen it.*
*The one who plays this symphony*
*understands its harmony—*
*the one who listens to its melody*
*is the softness of the sound.*
*Indeed, the one who reads this book aloud*
*is the One who has written it,*
*for Deity, its Self-Awareness*
*and all it perceives*
*are one perfect Identity.*

*This is your Melody,*
*dear woodcutter who is King.*
*Reign with Childlikeness!*
*Lift up your Heart and sing!*

# 19: Your Task

## Silence Ends the Search, by Bob Harwood

At the age of twenty, I became consumed with a wide range of existential questions. Is there a God? What is the meaning of life? What is a subatomic particle? What could explain the observer paradoxes in modern physics? In an effort to answer these kinds of questions, I spent ten years studying philosophy and science and doing a lot of thinking. During those ten years I never found a single answer. At the age of thirty, I discovered Zen, and I spent the next ten years reading Zen books and thinking about koans and enlightenment. During those ten years, I added a lot of questions to my list, but I never found a single answer. At the age of forty, my optimism waned and I began to feel like a rat in a trap. I worried that I might die without ever learning anything important. Fortunately, some business problems put me under a lot of stress, and in an effort to acquire some peace of mind, I started doing a simple breath awareness exercise.

After doing the exercise for a week, I realized that when I watched my breath, I was interacting with the world differently than when I pursued abstract thought. I therefore increased my practice to two hours each day. After two months, I increased my practice to three hours each day. After five months, I began falling into deep states of samadhi. Soon thereafter I had my first mind-blowing enlightenment experience.

After that first experience, I realized that everything I was searching for could be found through silent awareness. For the next fifteen years I went on silent retreats and solo hikes in the mountains. Gradually, the answers to my questions appeared. At the age of fifty-five only one question remained. I wondered how it was possible to remain in a unified state of mind following an enlightenment experience. During the previous fifteen years I had had many enlightenment experiences. Some of those experiences had been shallow and some had been deep. Some had been so deep that I stayed in a selfless and empty state of mind

225

for several days thereafter. Some had been so deep that it took months before the effects wore off. Some effects never wore off. Nevertheless, sooner or later I always seemed to return to a dualistic state of mind—a "me-in-here" looking at a "world-out-there." I thought that surely there must be some way "to make the two become one" forever.

On August 17, 1999 I was hiking up a mountain in Colorado when I had yet another experience of psychological unity. A few hours afterwards, I was surprised to realize that my 35-year-long spiritual search had come to an end. I knew the answer to my final question. I realized that there had never been a "me" who was sometimes psychologically unified and sometimes divided. I realized that who I was was the dynamic, mysterious, and intellectually unknowable field of reality itself. Although there had seemed to be a separate "me" who periodically became unified with reality, this had been an illusion. There was no "me." There was only oneness—only what is. Who I am was THAT!

My lifelong search had been based upon a fundamental error created by reflective thought. After seeing the truth clearly, I was free. I was never again bothered by any kind of existential question, and I was finally able to relax and live an ordinary life. From that time until today, I have known that wherever I look I am looking at myself—a unified field of being. The observer and the observed are one. Yes, I momentarily manifest as a particular human being, but my True Self is infinite—beyond space and time. Who I am has never been born and will never die.

Most people think that I am a separate human being, but they are dreaming the same dream that I used to dream. If they want to see the real me, then they must stop thinking and become silent. The secret of all secrets is that there is no secret. Everything lies in plain sight. If you don't see it, then be patient and be persistent. Jesus taught his disciples two parables about the importance of persistence. Keep looking. Stay silent. Sooner or later the truth will appear.

## Struggling Blindly, by Art Ticknor

Struggling blindly
in the fog of beliefs,
you grasp first one then another
in the quest for security.

What you seek lies between and behind these beliefs.
I am the respectful doubt,
the solvent that detaches beliefs.

Believe in Me.

## The Certainty You Seek, by Bob Cergol

*People who have had profound realizations frequently receive correspondence from others who refer to insights or experiences they've had, sometimes looking for confirmation and other times seeking guidance. The self-realized person tries to get a handle on the correspondent's perspective and convey something that may light the fuse for a deeper realization. - Ed.*

I think you are seeing directly what you are—or rather the fixation of the attention on the object-experience of "Dave" is dissolving—and is instead itself becoming the object of its own attention. The man in the theatre, so engrossed in watching the movie of experience—by virtue of a power of attention that does not belong to him—loses his focus on the movie, and in that instant awareness recognizes itself as the only Being—leaving the poor man in the theatre behind. This leads to much consternation and machinations in the mind of the man in the theatre!

You can lose the immediacy of an experience, you can lose a verbalization of something you witnessed. You cannot lose the realization of what you are—provided that realization was not dependent upon experience and verbalizations. The experiences that people talk and write about are reactions by and of the individual to the realization. Quite a paradox.... Quite inexplicable....

Realization is not an intellectual conclusion. The intellectual conclusions are after-the-fact reactions belonging to the relative mind. There are those who claim they achieved Self-Realization as a result of an intellectual path. It could also be that their path was one of direct inward looking, unbeknownst to them, and that all the intellectual machinations that accompanied it were mere reactions and did not involve any doing by the individual whatsoever and were of no consequence.

You want a certainty that you don't have. The character on the stage that is animated and illuminated by Awareness remains on that stage exactly as before the magic occurs—the magic being Awareness manifesting as separate individuality bends back upon unmanifested Awareness—and Awareness as a drop knows itself to be Awareness as the ocean. The stage remains. The mind remains. Thoughts continue. So long as the machinery is in motion, it will continue to operate according to its characteristics and history.

Who is this character that conceives that the character needs to be remade?

You have, in the very conflict you state, the immediate occasion to look directly. If you truly have realized, then such looking will "reconnect" you with that realization, and if your realization is merely relative, then such looking can transcend that and provide the certainty you need and want.

I lived very close to Richard Rose and knew him very well. His was a difficult personality to interact with. He told me once that people had such absurd ideas about the requirements of personality for reaching a spiritual realization. He said a whore-master could get enlightened, and that after enlightenment, he would still be a whore-master—only free of the attachment. His point was that the egocentricity of perspective people carry *is* the block and that it is the

relinquishing—nay the removal—of that egocentric perspective that opens the blinds, permanently. A change *will* be manifest in that person's character and actions—but not necessarily witnessed by others according to their expectations. Being free of Karma does not mean that the law of cause-and-effect ceases to manifest in the dream. It might mean that new Karma is not created. Rather a moot distinction for the person sitting in the theatre watching the movie play out.

I think the formula is simply "daily remembrance"—meaning a habit of inward looking: seeing, *not* thinking (that happens all by itself anyway). It is the seeing, or attempt to see, that is important. Visualization is not seeing. Therefore oblique looking is effective. That oblique looking is looking at conflict. All conflict is an affliction to the sense of self and opens the connection in a timeless instant for one to see directly what one is, one's Source, but the individual *immediately* looks away. That looking away is experienced as the onrush of emotions and thoughts that provide a substitute object for the attention. This is tricky in that you cannot just sit and attempt to make your mind blank. You have to look at something. You cannot look at nothing. The way to ask the "Who Am I?" question is to ask it obliquely by recalling afflictions to the sense of self. The attention splits—a piece of it stares directly into that very sense of self and from whence it arises—another piece spins off in reaction. Eventually the latter collapses in on itself leaving only what's left when that self, or sense of self, falls away: NOTHING of you remains. And that somehow brings certainty to the individual who lives this life—amid the largely same set of circumstances and attendant problems.

## Inner Guidance, by Jim Burns
### Three excerpts from *At Home with the Inner Self*

You may unconsciously be chastising yourself that inner work is not a good use of time and energy. You may be prejudiced against your own thinking compared to what someone else says or what you read in a book. You have to think as much of your own thoughts as you do of somebody else's. You may feel foolish about the things you are thinking about, but you have to start somewhere. You have to realize that you are trying to be a student of yourself and that it is a good effort.

*x*

Starting as a child you seek guidance outside yourself because you know no better and you don't have the brain to even imagine being a source of your own guidance. Everyone wants to belong, and when you are a child you want to belong to all the idiots who don't think, which is the whole crux of the problem. Ultimately your own system is the guidance you're seeking and is perfectly attuned to your circumstances.

*x*

I was stumbling around with meditation and discovered that if something was bothering me and an answer to the problem occurred to me, then it stopped bothering me. So when something started bothering me I knew I was looking for a specific answer, which was the golden key to the thing. Little did I realize how much work it would be. At first you don't know what you are seeking. Once you make the discovery of this inner satisfaction, then you know what you are seeking for. You're blind to it for quite a while. You just know things aren't what you'd like, but you aren't able to be specific about it. Our major appetite is the need to comprehend. Comprehension is a specific appetite and even needs to understand itself. You need to know what the mind is trying to get done so you can be more effective at it. Your internal system is entirely capable, given the opportunity, to teach you what it is trying to teach you. Your inner being knows. Your outer being is always unknowing.

## Do What You Say, by Shawn Nevins

You should not underestimate the importance of a simple step. Here is an easily overlooked practice that will set you on the road to spiritual discovery: *Do what you say you will do.*

An example: you agree to meet someone at 9:00 AM. You either will or will not. If you do not, you have either an unavoidable or an avoidable excuse. You may have a flat tire from a nail, or a flat tire because you neglected to get a leak repaired. One is avoidable and one is not. An avoidable excuse is used to soften the blow to your self-image that would occur if you admitted your lie.

You lied because a new desire-self arose later in the day, and overruled your well-intentioned commitment (which required making sure your transportation was reliable). Or you lied to your self in order to please another—part of you knowing all along you couldn't meet them. Either way, you have not observed or understood what you are. Especially if you believe such mundane commitments are not part of the spiritual path.

You are what you do, not what you believe—until you discover otherwise.

You will not discover otherwise unless you are truthful in both word and deed.

Of course, you can sit on your hands and make no commitments, thus avoiding the whole messy issue. Thus becoming a powerless creature of no-action.

Or you can discover the power of commitment and the action it necessitates. By funneling this action into a continual pursuit of truth through the observation of egoistic poses and facades, you eventually unveil the source of all power, action, and life.

## Your Task, by Hakuin Zenji (1689-1796)

The self is simply a bundle of perceptions. Perceptions themselves, their organs, and things perceived are without substance, as the Heart Sutra tells us. Yet at the same time, the self is the agent of realization and the setting of serious practice. The Buddha pointed out that it is difficult to be born a human being and difficult then to find the Buddha Dharma. Indeed. When you reflect on the infinite number of happenstances that coalesced to produce you, then you understand how unique, how precious, how sacred you really are. Your task is to cultivate that precious, sacred nature and help it to flower.

When a guru's not engaged in meditation
A-reciting of his mantra for the week,
His capacity for infantile inflation
Is enough to drive disciples up the creek.
He will take the girls aside for tantric yoga
While celibacy's ordered for the chaps;
If he starts behaving like an angry ogre
He will claim it's just to make your pride collapse.
Oh, with all this yogic practice to be done,
A disciple's lot is not a happy one.

*This poem by John Wren-Lewis was inspired by "The
Policemen's Chorus" from* The Pirates of Penzance
*and the first (1988) edition of* The Serpent Rising *by
Mary Garden.*

# 20: REFLECTIONS

## *Our State of Mind: The Ring that Binds, by Bob Fergeson*

We all go through life maintaining our belief system, or state of mind, to the point of controlling everything in sight, so as to keep the ego of body and mind alive and well. This will hold even in the face of death, for we would rather be right than admit our error and live with it. We also grant our fellow man this same hell by forcing him to be as we, even if it means controlling his every action, all in order to keep our precious ego afloat. To grant ourselves freedom, eternal and infinite, we must do the same for everyone else, and leave the hypnotic ring of attachment to the ego of body and mind. Through the clear examination of our very "selves," and those of our friends, we break the ring and find freedom in simple awareness. This is how we become, and in so becoming, free ourselves from the chains of mind and ego.

Most of us base our relationships on unexamined belief systems, and see others as merely things to be manipulated, hypnotized, and brought into that system, as we were. We don't see each other as real, but as objects either in our belief system, and thus right and in the proper place in the system's hierarchy, or as threat-objects to the system, which must be changed or removed. Thus, people are either acceptable recruits for our personal state of mind or are heretics and should be attacked. This is all to keep our ego afloat, for if we are to be right, our beliefs must be upheld by not only our own mind, but by everyone else's as well. Thus, we cannot question ourselves, which is the same as coming to know ourselves, for that would call the whole belief system into jeopardy.

Most states of mind involve the application of pressure to keep us running in the circle of body and mind. We feel a certain pressure, perhaps coming through the body, as a need for a certain pleasure. The mind is then used to rationalize the pressure-releasing act. The mind can also be the initial source of the pressure. We may have an irrational fear, never really questioned but now a habit, which the mind forces on the body, causing it to perform irrational actions. These circular patterns of behavior and rationalization tie up our energy and direction, negating any real spiritual progress. We are left trapped in a world of inner fantasy and imagination as concerns our inner journey, for the real motivations of our daily life are left to forces of direction other than our own. These forces then use us as agents to recruit our friends into whatever peculiar trap with which we have become enamored, creating another ring of attachment and descent.

How can we escape from this ring, this trap of identification with the dominant state of mind of our body-ego? Ruysbroeck points to the path to freedom when he tells us of the differences between the Servants of God, His Friends, and His Sons. Each step along the inward path requires more and more objectivity to the very thing we know the least about: our very "self." The hidden must be revealed, whether we believe in it or not. Each step along the path from Servant to Son requires a lessening of attachment to objects, whether these objects are people, desires, fears, or our own manifestation as an apparent body/mind. The Servant deals in the world of objects, serving his conception of the higher good through the manipulation of these objects according to his beliefs. As these beliefs are questioned and called into the light of discrimination, the seeker becomes less attached to objects, and moves inward towards the formless. His progress is helped by those above him, the true spiritual Friends, who see clearer than he, and grant him the freedom to become as they.

One way to see the hidden but dominant state of mind that runs our life is to observe how the trap of unconscious belief works in our friends. It is much easier to see the irrational habits, desires and fears in those around us, for it is not so threatening to our own ego. The mistakes, rationalizations and contradictory behavior of those familiar to us can be used as a door to our own mind. We may begin to see how our relationships are based on mutual neediness, in keeping similar states of mind afloat. If we are lucky, we may have the intuition that the imperfections in our friends are much the same as those hiding in us. This can be a frightening thought, for once we see clearly the traps of body and mind that snare our friends, we get the hint that we, too, are just as unconsciously snared.

By taking this simple step within, and realizing that we are asleep to our basic motivations and drives, we lessen their hold on us, and become less attached. Most attachments are dependent on a mental image, usually that of a state or object which we wish to possess, coupled with the ego's illusion that we are in control and know what we are doing. Through questioning our desire or fear of these mind-objects, we become a little freer, and self is a bit diminished.

In moving within, to a state of mind less attached to the systems of desire and fear, of energy loss and objects, we come to move in a straight line, rather than in the downward spiral of the blind leading the blind. From this straighter path leading within, we can also help those of similar bent. If we have no pressure forcing us to change the world of objects, having lost our attachment to them, we will no longer treat our friends as objects, and thus grant them the freedom to move within also. We may begin to get hints that they, too, are using us as examples of what states of mind can do, and are thus making progress through viewing our particular displays of folly.

Through the seeing of "self" in our friends, we may gradually come to see "self" in ourselves. This "fathomless staring and seeing" leads to the lessening of attachment to this "self" and its eventual demise through a startling discovery. We come to see that there are no separate "selves" or objects, including our own "self" or that of our friends, but only the Universal Awareness of Man.

## Poems by Shawn Nevins

Slipping silently from my mind
this sense of self, this life of mine.
My I-ness melts like film
burned by the projector's light —
the cold heat of eternity's doom.
I will not even raise my hand
to acknowledge my passing.
No, I will bow to my doom.
Trembling, I remember life's losses
and the shortfall of love within
the weak grasp of my self.
I remember my heart that aches
with uncertainty and longs for it knows not what.
I remember I am reaching down to my self,
that I-ness was a shadow of oneness,
that my care is as large as all being,
that God is me as surely as you.
God thinks to run, but for a moment,
as he too slides,
drawn by eternity's spiral
into quiet.
As for the quiet, I cannot speak across that chasm.

Some words,
death for instance,
carry truth unimaginable.
Yet it rolls off the tongue
like a student of history recounting
what he's never seen.
Some words
take a lifetime to define.

"Sounds"

Hear these solitary notes reach out
across a deep lake of silence
that we do not understand.
Their longing sounds relax
and unfold our confusion,
as their inevitable fading
pulls us toward the silent wisdom
pouring between
every moment of our life.

~❧

Stillness speaks words more eloquent than I,
If only you will give up the idea
That I know more than you.
What you see is as dead as stone.

A teacher acts out his destiny
While the student misreads all the parts.
The student is but a teacher
Wearing a mask of fearful lies —
Blind to the script.

Follow my sad look, as sadness is the mark
Of beauty too painful for words,
Even as beauty is just a word
Floating in an empty canyon at twilight.

~❧

The last night,
the holy night,
when all resolves to a last goodbye
to all we hold close.
A night of leaving our believing
in life as a field of connections.
Tonight, severing connections,
we bow down before the last fear of aloneness
and toss our glass into oblivion,
whispering sweet nothingness.

The seed is not the source.
Finding the "I Am,"
the seed finds itself.

Motion flings you outward,
but the gravitational pull of silence
brings you home.
"I Am," the seed, is the orbital balance point.

Walk in the right direction,
following your hunger.

The world moves:
jays crisscross the sky,
clouds stretch across a blue expanse,
roosters call across the hills
and rise to the challenge of life.
An old hound bellows,
reminding himself of his self,
and the grass sways in tune with sing-song warblers.

Yet every sound slides across solid ice,
every response is a reflection in glass,
and our soul,
*the* soul,
is infinitely wide and deep,
smooth and still.

## *Are You a Person? by Art Ticknor*

Then you will be alternately happy and unhappy. The fun prospects of life are ruined by death waiting in the wings. Of course death may eventually seem appealing. You will never be fully satisfied. An individual (a separate thing) is never going to be *whole.*

Ramana Maharshi stated his view succinctly: "'I am a man' is not natural. You are neither this nor that." Nisargadatta Maharaj put it even more forcefully: "You have squeezed yourself into the space of a lifetime and the volume of a body, and thus created the innumerable conflicts of life and death. Have your being outside this body of birth and death, and all your problems will be solved. They exist because you believe yourself born to die. Undeceive yourself and be free. You are not a person!"

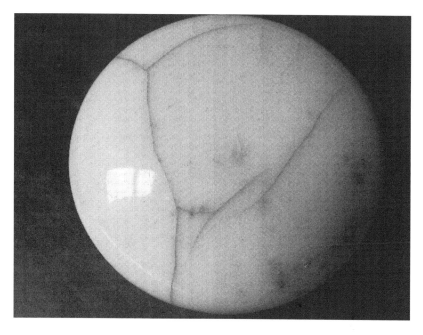

"Undeceive yourself and be free." Indeed. And what are the self-deceptions that need to be shaken loose? The outer layers of the onion of self-deception are our identification with desires and fears. We misidentify with the desire for acceptance, love, approval, status, wealth, security, fame, making a difference, being remembered, and so on. And we are hypnotically attached to the fear of rejection, appearing foolish, being wrong, making a blunder, being laughed at, censure, condemnation, social banishment, annihilation. When we introspect the mind, the war of desires and fears will come into perspective from a superior point of observation. It will become obvious to us that the fears and desires are objects in our view, not the subject or viewer.

The next layer of self-deception is that of being the doer, the decider, the person calling the shots. Again, watching the mind and observing mental processes will dispel the layer of self-deception. We don't know how to "do" this, but effort in the direction of self-observation results in an apparent accident which bumps our point of reference to a higher or more interior level of observation.

Since anything that's in our view is not us, the yet-to-be-defined viewer, we have at this point unwittingly reduced our self-definition to that of a possibly featureless but separate observer-thing. To proceed, our intuition must tell us that we somehow have to observe the observer—a logical impossibility. So how can we bring that about?

I heard the screen and stage star Matthew Broderick being interviewed recently, and he knew the formula. One of the interviewer's questions was about the timing of the events that led to his being discovered. He said that he'd been working off-Broadway for years without recognition. He was in the final night's performance of a play, which a well-known critic attended. The critic was impressed and wrote a glowing review. Broderick summarized: "All these things have to line up, which are out of your control." By persevering, you bring yourself to a place where discovery may occur.

## *The Circle Where Nothing Grows, by Gary Harmon*

In every dimension is a place where nothing will grow
When we leave this earth meet me there
I will gravitate to that spot where we stood before
I long for the place that is an abyss to all
Only weeds grow there, no trees will survive
They call this the place where nothing grows
As I walk through this circle of nothingness once again
A smell is noticed that is unrecognizable but familiar
I have stood on this spot before with my friend, my teacher
There arises recognition, a remembrance, a knowing
We have met here before and will meet here again
No movement, no time, no space, no we
Only that which is where nothing will grow

## The Procedure Toward Awakening, by Alfred Pulyan

Normally the procedure toward "awakening" goes something like this:

STAGE (1) // Battered by the storms of life or driven by an interior compulsion or even some "experience" a person becomes dissatisfied with his or her current religion (or the lack of it), and drifts and studies such things as Unity, Theosophy, Christian Science, maybe even Rosicrucianism, Zen, etc. Possibly they will read Huxley's "Perennial Philosophy" & dip into Far Eastern texts now so easily available. They may get the idea that there is a thing called liberation or awakening or satori or realization, although it seems extremely vague and their passion for miracles & marvels gets mixed up with it.

STAGE (2) // Sooner or later the "master-" or "guru-" idea comes up since the student gets nowhere by himself or herself usually. To "pick" a master or guru, cold turkey, is not at all easy because there are not enough available for picking & choosing. However there are the correspondence courses, the Essene Society, the Brotherhood of Light, etc. etc. (I make up names although I may have guessed an actual name—it does not matter.)

I often wonder whether some of these are not genuine & could actually do the job! However, the attention one gets, needs to be *far more individualized & personal* because this is not "learning," it is partly a transmission through friendship or love. One does not usually *sell these* things. Then there are the Swamis of the Vedanta Society, very well educated & high-toned men indeed & they conduct yoga classes. There is a Zen master in New York at the First Zen Institute. Here we touch more satisfactory gurus. The question of "how long" each of these takes is to be considered & of course these do NOT "work" *by mail*. Is there any genuine guru who does?

The student may meet by good luck (if that is the proper word) a master, such as a rare one in the Taoist succession or some other kind. (There are people in USA belonging to NO sect, cult or religion who "work" as I do, suiting my vocabulary to the student's habits. Again, few work *by mail* if any.)

The student by now is *getting a good idea* (even though he is not "awakened") of what he wants & how to judge. Remember I am speaking of personal interviews. He may drift from guru to guru (all good) until he reaches one that really suits him.

Meanwhile it is assumed that the student has gradually become more & more familiar with the "Perennial Philosophy" or "Wisdom Religion" (or whatever term you use to describe what Honoré Morrow puts into the mouth & mind of her character Lincoln). It becomes clear that "awakening" consists of realizing that we have come from & return to this One Self (to speak crudely perhaps). *At this stage* the student is said to "dip one toe in the ocean," i.e. to accept the general theory or doctrine and be ready to accept "work."

STAGE (3) // I do not wish to go into the whole technique of work with a guru but one thing is clear.

The student realizes that "awakening" or "realization" will never come unless at least once the student has surrendered the "boss-concept" of ego or self, the idea that it is a Supreme Court in itself, self-sufficient, "Captain of My Soul" (as Henley boasts & poor Bertrand Russell squeaks after him) —

Since the student is seeking to realize "that" to which he is subordinate, second-in-command, it is obvious he must lower his flag, admit his lower status, at some time.

It is extremely easy for one person even like you to hold the great "God" (so-called) of the Universe AWAY. *One little finger suffices.* Even a penny can hide the Sun. Thus without your active cooperation, & agreement to do as your guru says, there is not even a ghost of a chance of realization. If the student wishes to "win" he should not be a student because it is hard enough when both guru and student are eagerly cooperating! Such a "win" is a Pyrrhic victory—it is *far too easy.*

Thus in Japan the applicant must wait outside the gates of the monastery a day or so. It is done rather symbolically now—once it was very real & the applicant was repulsed, treated roughly, told to go away & the gate slammed in his face.

But nowadays with Ipana toothpaste with Hexa-Hexa-Hexachlo-rophene & innumerable detergents competing over TV [the applicant] wants to be wooed, gently persuaded, urged to enter—and the $1,000,000 bill must be washed & ironed & handed over on a silken cushion before he will accept it.

## *Transmission, by Bart Marshall*

In Zen, the word *transmission* is used to denote the "passing on" of enlightenment through a master-student relationship. It is mislead-ing, in that it implies an energy transference in which enlightenment flows from someone who "has" it to someone who does not.

Still, there's really no better word for what Zen points at with *transmission*. Enlightenment cannot be "taught" like mathematics or language, or mastered with "practice," like art or music. The Zen master's task is more akin to helping someone born with no sense of humor suddenly break into an uncontrollable belly laugh. Or to trigger in a self-absorbed ego-maniac a spontaneous experience of unconditional love. One never makes "progress" towards this sort of thing. It could happen any moment, or never. And so when Truth stands revealed, it is said *transmission* has occurred.

Within that metaphor, however, it is perhaps more accurate to say that transmission is occurring *always*. God, Tao, the One, the Source, the Absolute—whatever we might call it—is in an unceasing state of transmission. Awakening is when *reception* occurs. (Although this, too, is misleading since there is no *receiver*.)

God's eternal state of transmission is a standing "invitation to receive" that may be accepted at any moment—but not by the ego-identity. The ego-mind—even one that has spent years "seeking enlightenment"—treats the invitation to receive transmission as a threat, as "the hound of heaven." As long as ego is in control—or *believes itself to be*—the hound is successfully kept at bay. But if ego is dethroned for even a moment, the hound is upon it, and its name is Grace. Invitation accepted, transmission complete.

Knowing the ego-identity to be the sole "guardian of the gate," the Zen master—with the permission and complicity of the aspirant—goes about the business of undermining and attacking its "authority" in subtle, and sometimes not-so-subtle, ways.

This is the *entire* work of Zen. There is no teaching or practice, no zapping, no secret wisdom imparted with words—or rather, whatever there is of this is not the point. The Zen master is up to one thing only—the maneuvering of the seeker's ego-mind into a sufficiently vulnerable position that it might falter just long enough for *reception* to occur.

The master transmits nothing. He does not "have" enlightenment (no one ever has) so what could he transmit? He is a midwife, a facilitator, an "awakening therapist."

All rests with the aspirant. The Source is as unavoidable as air—the very "space" you now take in. How close is the place you peer out from? How far from it could you stray? To "see" it where do you look? To "know" it where do you go?

It's very hard to make predictions, particularly about the future. ~ *Yogi Berra*

If I have any beliefs about immortality, it is that certain dogs I have known will go to heaven, and very, very few persons. ~ *James Thurber*

I wouldn't fear death at all if I didn't have to be there at the time. ~ *Woody Allen*

You'd be surprised how much it costs to look this cheap. ~ *Dolly Parton*

Photons have mass? I didn't even know they were Catholic. ~ *Stephen Wright*

# 21: Desires

### *Desires, by Shawn Nevins*

We are all driven. I maintain that if you peel away the layers of reason and feeling, you discover that the philosophic mysteries drive our actions. Who or what am I? why am I here? and what happens when I die? are a few of these uncertainties. These questions are answerable by you in this lifetime. That few people find answers is due to the amount of honest thought and effort they apply. To succeed in any endeavor requires you to turn your back upon other possibilities. Not forever, perhaps, but until you attain your true goal. A professional chef who also wants to be a professional musician finds that one or the other profession suffers.

The pursuit of my deepest desire demanded I turn my back upon careers and romantic relationships. Immediately some of you will react negatively to that. What is required is to balance our desires, you say. Well, you can try to juggle three flaming torches, or you can hold one steadily and light your way with it [cf. "Finding Balance" in the *Nov. 2001 Forum*]. Even with the freedom of youth, this turning away and choosing one torch was difficult. Most people's entire life, their meaning, is defined by work and family. What gives them definition also consumes their life's energy. I had a number of career opportunities and a wonderful relationship and was torn between commitments many times. At these moments of decision, I found a way to ensure honesty in my choice.

The method was to ask, "Where is this decision taking me? Who will I be when all is said and done?" I imagined being an old man on his deathbed. In one ending I, the old man, looked back upon a life of accomplishments. A wonderful family perhaps, or wealth, or fighting to save the planet. Even allowing that I played the game of life perfectly and escaped unscathed, I was deeply disappointed. All I was and had done would fade away. Alone, in the face of my final moment, what I truly wanted was clear.

I wanted the alternate ending—to spend my life seeking an answer. The answer was unimaginable, and even if I didn't find it, seeking was the only game that held the hope of certainty—the answer that would settle my soul.

With this method, you think through various life possibilities and prevent following numerous desires only to find them ultimately unsatisfying. Models of how to spend your life surround you. Ask yourself if that is how you want to end up. What could be more unsatisfying than to die ignorant of what should be most certain—your essence, your soul? Even with that thought, though, you still spin other dreams. Like a friend who had cancer told me, "Even though I know

I have cancer, I still find myself turning on the TV, wasting time. You forget." As other desires arise, return to this thinking-through method to reinforce your deepest desire.

Once, while desperately frustrated with my spiritual search, I said to Richard Rose, "If I could think of some other place to go, I would." I wanted to give up what, at the time, seemed an impossible task. I imagined burying myself in life's details. I thought through every possible life I could live, other than the search. Only the interior search offered hope of dispelling the mystery and fear, and shedding light on the inkling of profundity I sensed inside. Every path other than the search was a play—a play whose stars were ignorant of the play's purpose and of existence beyond the stage. Every other path eventually ran out and left me facing the mystery of life and the self.

Yet I wonder if there are some roles we must play in order to discard them. I've known people who half-heartedly followed a spiritual path while, let's say, longing to walk in a beautiful meadow. They may even fear imagined snakes in the meadow or feel guilty for having the longing, yet their mind returns again and again to thoughts of the meadow. For example, if you have never fallen in (and out) of love, you may never willingly turn your back upon the possibility that a relationship would assuage your inner longing. Of course, there are longings other than philosophic ones pushing you to explore romantic love (a welter of lust, pride, fear, and selfless friendship). Clearly seen in action, such drives reveal the need for a deeper resolution.

So a certain amount of success and disappointment with the world is required, yet as much as possible you want to avoid poking your head into every oven only to discover it is as hot as the previous one. Time is running out. Think your way through desires instead of exploring every one. You may fear missing out, but billions have gone down those other roads before you and never returned. Unimaginable possibilities await.

## Poems by Shawn Nevins

A bell rings, blown in the wind.
There is no one there to hear it
And never was.

Yet I hear it ringing;
Hear the sound of Reality.

All I ever wanted spills at my feet
As desire itself unravels
And reason-for-being melts into
Simple fear of dissolution.

In the blackest abyss is Singular Life —
Singular Presence.
Past these words I cannot take you,
But speak from them without fear.

❧

A cloud empties itself
upon the earth.
Fields shine beneath a clear sky.
Whatever passed by the window of my eye,
I no longer care.

❧

Death is:
the mind curling in upon itself,
the head and tail of time
engulfing one another,
and what remains after the moment
when Pulyan's penny no longer blocks the sun.

❧

A crow and a human voice
sound no different
down here by water's edge.
Both lay claim
to what is not theirs.
There is an ever present edge
in everything we do —
a frightening peace
lapping between our words.

These words are a prayer answered.
Take out pen and paper
and pray upon them.
Let God answer
through your heart and hand.
Those words are the source of creation
and are gold compared to these.

When life in us and around us is so full,
how do we remember our longing?
Like puppies playing in a sun-drenched field,
growing by the moment
we put everything in our mouth.

Listen to your voice receding into silence.
Feel the touch and leaving of your friends.
Be the last to leave the field.
Stand and watch the dying light of day.
Hear the fading sounds of companionship.
A new life begins in emptiness.

## *Milk From Thorns, by Wilma Holmes*

I do think there is a difference in the paths to spiritual contentment dependent on one's gender. However, I also think there are variations within that continuum based on individual differences.

I've heard that Mr. Rose often told women to have children rather than to remain childless. However, he always told me: "Live the spiritual life. Don't get married. Don't have children. The spiritual life is a beautiful life." I think I heard that once every six weeks. Up to this point I have only half listened, and it has worked very well for me.

I got married to someone who was already pretty far along on a spiritual path, so there is a certain spiritual compatibility. It is not what Mr. Rose prescribed, yet after a month-long isolation, I determined that the marriage thing wasn't going to let me go until I answered to it. It has worked out wonderfully and has never been anything but a help to my path.

As an intuitive versus a logical woman, I have found that not having children has been the most helpful thing to my path that I could ever have done. I find that a work environment versus a home-child environment helped me build the parts of my mind that were not as developed as the emotional-intuitive aspects. It allowed me to better become a process observer and to isolate the watcher.

However, I know from many logical women that having children helped them develop their more emotional-intuitive (the right side of Jacob's ladder) side in ways that they otherwise wouldn't have. Mr. Rose used to say that one had to become both man and woman to get there. I don't have a large enough sample size though to conduct a scientifically sound study on this.

Next to the big question of whether to have children or not, there are other parts of a woman's path that differ from a man's. For one, women have a cycle each month that men do not. That means that the hormones and therefore the thought patterns are shifting all month long for women. I have found this to be a tremendous advantage. However, initially, it was the only reason that I didn't know if I would make it as a seeker. It was horrible to overcome. Maybe it is the same trouble that men have with celibacy. For women, the desire to have children is built in by nature through a monthly cycle. It can be debilitating for a spiritual path in the beginning, and each month I found that I went from seeking to wanting to have children back to seeking.

Days 1-5 I was sad that I didn't have children, and days 12-14 I was interested in finding a mate to have children. I found Day 15 to be somewhat depressing, when the hormone levels drop after ovulation, since pregnancy was not in sight. Days 21-28 I was only interested in seeking an answer. Each month I went round and round.

Mr. Rose suggested keeping a journal to see how my thinking tracked the hormone cycle, and I distinctly remember eight months after starting it that, when I read back over the previous eight months, I saw that I had the same thoughts the same time of the month for eight months. I remember crying and writing in my journal that I was just a big ol' hormone cycle and nothing more.

However, after six years of watching the cycle and trying not to get sucked in, the clock finally stopped ticking. I had a profound experience in which I realized that all I had to do was follow God's will and nothing more in life and that all wouldn't just be okay, it would be miraculous. At that moment, my clock stopped ticking, and I just worked on listening and following. No more clock causing me a problem. This was a major step forward on my path as it was the end of my wanting to have children.

The advantage to the cycle is that if used strategically, it can be a boon in terms of spiritual insight and experience that makes the cycle more valuable than not having it. For example, days 1-5 provide the optimal times for intuition to occur naturally. Since they appear to be the days where intuition meets logic in perfect balance, I find that days 16-19 are optimal for thinking over difficult concepts. Days 21-27 are the most logical days when I can view any issue in terms of cold hard logic with little emotion, which can be helpful for different parts of the path.

Mr. Rose used to always say "milk from thorns." I think a woman's cycle is the one thing that keeps women from pursuing philosophical truths. However, when used with a little insight, the cycle can provide many different states of mind in which to view one's spiritual path and issues each month. I find that superior to not having a cycle back when I was 12.

### *The River, by Art Ticknor*

The Ohio River flows
along where I walk most days.
It begins in Pittsburgh,
formed by the confluence

of two rivers there,
then meanders for nearly
a thousand miles
before flowing into the

Mississippi, which in turn
flows for about another
eleven hundred miles before
merging into the ocean.

What is a river?
Without the water
it is a dry abstraction,
a mere concept.

A river with no water:
no-river.
A mind with no thought:
no-mind.

## Trusting the Inner Self, by Bob Fergeson

**Trap: Identification with pain.** The usual reaction to pain is avoidance, either through distraction or medication-induced relief. Thinking it is "us" that hurts, we must get rid of our pain. Pain is nothing more than a signal that something needs our attention. Identification with our thoughts and feelings, and thus our pain, keeps us from this simple truth. By avoiding pain or medicating it out of our awareness, we procrastinate facing both the problem the pain is pointing to and the action or change needed to solve it.

**Trick: Seeing pain for what it is.** By seeing pain as the simple signal it is, we can turn our attention on it without fear or overreaction. The underlying problem can be dealt with and, usually, the pain stops. This is especially true in relation to psychic pain, the avoiding of which can keep us in the following **Trap** of

**Ignoring our conscience:** That faint voice from the depths is often seen as a pain to be avoided, thus preventing us from learning the following **Trick** of

**Trusting the Inner Self:** If we learn to listen to this inner voice, our own inner wisdom, we see that instead of it being a pain or inhibition keeping us from what we want, it is actually a guiding signal from an interior compass deep within. This beacon gives us direction in our search, pointing to a path or lifestyle that gives better probability of Becoming. Experience will show that the pang of conscience is best dealt with by the *avoidance of temptation, not pain.*

> "Man does not know the influences which cause him to think and to act, as long as he does not know his own nature. He is therefore not a responsible being, except to the extent of his wisdom and power to control his own nature. Wisdom and strength can only be attained in life by experience and by the exercise of the power of overcoming temptation." - Franz Hartmann

Why women live longer than men....

# 22: To Die While Alive

## *Dear Aging Becomer, by Bob Cergol*

You consider yourself more esoterically informed than most—way, way ahead of the common masses and "Joe-six-pack." You think because you have known a teacher, digested a lot of books, engaged in ascetic practices, performed good works, held meetings, meditated, or prayed—that you have become a more spiritual person through these actions. You think that you are earning your reward and that you have become something more than you were before. (Bit by bit, a little better each and every day, step by step, better and better in every way.) You also feel, that your failure to "do" as much as you should have, and could have, explains why you haven't quite finished becoming—whatever it is that you are supposed to become, in order to cross that critical threshold—whereupon…. How long will it take you to become?

When did you start this becoming project? Did you start becoming only after you met your teacher? What did you *do* that was fundamentally different than before you met your teacher?

Your teacher told you, "You are what you do." *Are you?* Are you defined by what you do? When you eat too much and move too little, you become fat. When you eat less and move more, you become thin—and hungry…. This is your paradigm: Doing is becoming. When you can no longer do—what will you be? What were you before you could "do"? It seems that you simply appeared one day and started doing, started on your way to becoming you, and then, way, way down the road, decided that you would "do" differently in order to become more than you. Differently how?—a new diet of different thoughts and different experiences….

Can you remember, consciously, the day that you arrived and started becoming?

Well, shortly thereafter…. You interacted with your world and others and you became connected. You learned and practiced things and you became capable. You were stroked and affirmed and you became loving—and self-centered. You were offended and you became angry. You were hurt and you became fearful. Your body grew and your experiences accumulated and you matured. According to the ebb and flow of your circumstances, you became confident and happy or diffident and depressed. You didn't see this happening, just as you don't see a plant growing. *You were always on the "resulting" side looking back.*

The ebb and flow in your moods left you feeling alone and vulnerable. You became aware that the process of becoming *you* was not unimpeded. You witnessed your relative weakness and found it unacceptable. Your awareness of your vulnerability called into question the very purpose of your becoming you—since you would apparently stop being you at some point. Your knowledge of this was reinforced 1,000 different ways as you died 1,000 petty deaths. So you became attracted to philosophies that promised a final solution to how you would overcome the impediments to your becoming you—forever. You were tantalized by the possibility of acquiring this final answer.

How long ago was that? What percentage of becoming have you completed? You're losing steam now, running out of breath. Is it because you're almost finished becoming you? Did you only think that you wanted "THE ANSWER"? Was it just some temporary need of a transitional you that you are no longer? Have your thoughts, emotions and actions simply been tracking that aging, withering body as though you yourself were nothing more than a side-effect?

Your teacher told you! *"You cannot learn [the Answer], you can only become [the Answer]."* This would have to mean that at the end of that becoming, you are the answer. Now that sure sounds like the best form of acquisition and possession you can imagine—one that cannot be taken away from you, no matter what. Not even death could steal a possession that was added to your very being.

In Rose's writings, and perhaps epitomized in his "Jacob's Ladder" diagram, he conveys his perspective that "The View is not the Viewer." He writes of a "somatic or body awareness" and of a "process-observer" or mental awareness, both of which are objects within "Absolute" or non-individualized Awareness.

If you can "be the truth" then how could you-the-false generate the Truth?! How can you the Shadow-Man, the view, possibly have created or generated the Viewer?! Here are the simple facts:

"That which is born dies. That which is never
born cannot die." - Nisargadatta
"Body and mind perish and are dissipated.
Nothing of you shall remain." - Pulyan

Is it possible that you have confused something you imagine as "change of being" with a mere change in your circumstances!?

How can you possibly believe that you can become that which is your source, or that lead can become gold—unless it were already of one and the same substance? How can you possibly become that which you already are? Was your teacher wrong? Or did you misunderstand him?

The answer to the paradox lies in defining the "YOU" of which I speak—and that you experience—and in remembering that Rose never defined the Truth that he said you could become. He only defined becoming as becoming a vector, and a reverse vector at that.

You thought you knew what that meant, but you haven't followed your teacher's advice. You haven't become anything of your own volition, least of all a reverse vector. You've continued along the same robotic path as when you met your teacher. Unwaveringly, you have spent your whole life worrying about and trying to become something— something that affirms and confirms your life and your individuality,

261

before the external world—not to mention Death!—puts an abrupt end to the whole endeavor and proves you wrong. You failed to notice that this experience you call living is in reality your reaction to the process of dying!—and that what you conceive and imagine as the process of dying and what you fear as death is in reality the process of discovering the only thing about you, or connected with you, that is alive!

You associate "doing" and "thinking" with living.

What is doing? Whatever it might be, whatever its source, it is something that you experience.

What is thinking? Whatever it is, whatever its source, it is something that you experience.

What is your life if you remove all doing and thinking? What's left?

Are you left with only "watching"?

Does that mean that life is basically "watching"?—that life is essentially an experience?

What is the vantage point of this "watching"? *Where are you?!*

*When you are watching, are you not also aware of being you—and watching? Isn't this awareness of being you, itself an experience being watched?*

Imagine you are paralyzed and the outside world perceives you as a vegetable because you cannot communicate in any way whatsoever and your body is powerless to maintain itself. What then are you watching? What of life would be left if you yourself were removed as an object to watch?

Your own death will be an event you watch—but for how long. You are already watching it daily. Your daily reaction is to look away, and the experience of looking away is your life of doing and thinking. Your body will die and be dissipated. Your mind, which is at all times one with that body will likewise be dissipated. Nothing of you will remain—as an object to be witnessed. *"Ashes to ashes, dust to dust, from dust were you made, and to dust shall you return."*

If that which you take as yourself, is itself a thought, an experience, and witnessed as such—what could possibly be left of you!?

That which you mis-take as your being, the "you," is itself merely an experience—tracking the body after the fact, as a reaction, as the experience of being the experience-er. Your attention is glued to, or fixated on, this outer experience—and the "you" I am referring to is definitely on the "outside," in the view, *and does not have an "attention."* Rather, you appear IN the attention and *ARE* that very power of Attention.

In the last 30 years, haven't you figured out—yet—how to become a reverse vector? Is it by more and more "doing" and "thinking"—by running faster and faster, in ever decreasing concentric circles—until … you become like the Do-Do Bird[1] Rose described. Is it through bodily action, or mental activity? Which of these follows which, and which is more substantial than Omar Khayam's "… snow upon the Desert's dusty Face, Lighting a little Hour or two—[and] gone"?

If death equates to the absence of doing, thinking and experiencing (i.e., nothing), then aren't you on your way to becoming nothing—with no effort required? Isn't that the direction of your life?

Can you actually become something, fundamentally different, than what you are right now? *Who or what is becoming?* You used to be convinced that you could become, now you only hope that you can, that this leaden "YOU" that you know and love so well—and hate—can become a golden you, that will deserve your love forever—and live forever—proving once and for all what in your heart you do not really believe—and most fear.

You the body-mind fantasize a vision of becoming something permanent, and superior to yourself—and that somehow you will remain anterior to everything—intact as "you"—containing God himself—the timeless.

## Where Did You Get Such a Delusion?!

I think it is your distorted seeing and hearing of the essential desire that comes to you from your true Self—your Essence—for even God does not have the power to split himself, and everything He touches was never separate from Him. (It is the Invisible Current from Rose's Jacob's Ladder diagram. This is pure metaphor, attempting to explain the mechanics of a creation that does not exist.)

You the Shadow-Man cannot fail to act in accordance with your essence, your true source and fundamental nature. However, your actions are refracted according to the fixation of your attention on experience, refracted according to the resulting need for self-definition and personal survival, and refracted according to the resulting fears and desires generated by the experience.

---

[1] Variously remembered by others as Foo Foo and Kufu, Rose humorously described this bird as flying in ever-decreasing circles until it eventually flew up its own rear and disappeared.

In other words, you the shadow man do not become or evolve or *will your* attention away from the false. You the shadow-man are watching two movies: one is the movie of your destruction, one is the movie of your denial and acceptance of this destruction. The theme of denial is depicted by the vision of becoming through acquisition. The theme of acceptance is depicted by one's own deconstruction through simple looking—with acceptance. Are you looking—or acquiring?

It is by virtue of your essence that your attention cannot be 100% glued to that which is separate. The desire and attempt to define your self, and to survive, is simply what manifests in the shadow of experience cast by the "Light of the body," that Christ said was "the eye." You, the Shadow-Man, are what manifests when Awareness reflects upon itself and finds no object to reflect upon.

Your attempt to become is doomed to failure. This is beautifully stated in these thematic and climactic phrases from the poem *The Hound of Heaven:*

> All things betray thee, who betrayest Me.
> Naught shelters thee, who wilt not shelter Me.
> Naught contents thee, who content'st not Me.
> All things fly thee, for thou fliest Me!
> Thou dravest love From thee, who dravest Me.

If your attempt to become transcendentally different is doomed to failure, what can and will you do about it?

Can your actions lead to a change in anything other than your circumstances? You believe that it can because you mistake the after-the-fact reactive experience as you-the-doer. It is *a wish* of you-the-somatic-mind.

Have you noticed that your actions have an effect upon your attention? What motivates your actions? The action of looking will further affect the focus of your attention.

Becoming a reverse-vector is the opposite of external, worldly becoming. It is un-becoming. It is your un-doing! It is the breaking of your fixation on all experience—including the experience of identity—until the attention collapses in upon itself and all experience either stops or is recognized as non-existent.

*Spiritual becoming is worldly and personal un-becoming through the reverse vector of the attention—"that power of noticing" which is not your* possession. The potential value in your activity aimed at becoming lies in the effect that it will have upon the direction of your attention—not in becoming something other than what you already are or are not.

Your desire to become was wisely exploited by your teacher, who coined the phrase: "milk from thorns." He also liked to recall the Radha Soami guru who answered his question about what can be done: "All that man can do is desire." Rose knew full-well the ultimate Source of this desire, and how this desire manifested in the "mind realm" and in the "body realm."

Your experience generates experience. *Experience is to the identity as food is to the body.*

Your identity weaves itself in a self-perpetuating chain-reaction— so long as the attention is glued to experience—and so long as the body fuels the reactor.

The "fabric" of identity unravels as the attention is turned to watching—first experience itself, as an outside observer rather than a participant, and then when the attention is turned to watching the experience-er.

Experience is binding.

Observing the process of experiencing is liberating.

Good hunting, and may your life experience be decidedly disconcerting.

As your faithful friend, I remain….

## *Poems by Shawn Nevins*

There are those who say the earth is hollow.
Are they mad geniuses or just mad?
Something is not quite right with the world
and madness is close to the mark, I say.
For it is not that upon which we stand that is hollow,
but that which we are.

Now, I hear
two voices —
the voice of life and of death.

Once, life was my whole
and its sound, my joy and sorrow.
Now, all my action is balanced with no action —
the board is continually erased.
Such a relief to be unconcerned with chalk dust.

I am written and erased —
the holy sound and silence.
I became honest, tired, and determined
in order to hear.

What is this vast emptiness
that gives me peace?
Across the plain of my mind
is bare space
and I have no will to write
of that which is not.
Only that which Is,
which is not me,
which I Am.

A plain peopled by one.
One who is transparent
to the eye of God.
God's eye that sees all things
and folds into itself,
revealing depths upon depths
expanding into nothingness.

This place is not my design,
yet it is me.
I have become the impersonal
and cannot look at anything
without being absorbed.
I see the smallest flower,
then that flower is me,
then stillness washes over us

draining color, life, and being.
Giving all that is unnameable.

I know this is vague.
Be quiet.
You are a drowned body floating in the sea
and a sea that watches,
dimly recalling the life of a man.

❧

"What I Was and What I Am"

I was all I dreamed and feared.
I was longing and confusion —
a puppy left by its master.

I am gale force winds that rip flesh from bone.
The space between all things
and the Fount.

Every word is corrupted by wordiness.
I am left behind and what is—Is.

❧

I look without the veil of words
and that look is vaster
than any thought of mine.
The desert is sparse and vast.
These words of ours are desert echoes.
What will be the call you hear?
A reflection, a glance, one unguarded moment
and all is known.

❧

What will you say to death?
That you disagree?
You need not accept or reject
the facts.
You will become what you must,
a little late, perhaps.

## Richard Rose on Controlling the Mind, by Art Ticknor
*From a presentation at the June 2006 TAT meeting*

D iscussing the technique that Richard Rose laid out in the final section of *The Psychology of the Observer* for bringing the mind under
control, I'd like to begin with a little survey to get your opinion:

Q: Do you feel you have some control over the mind? If so, what percentage, or what percentage of the time? If not, is your mind otherwise
controlled? Out of control?

This presentation is organized around fifteen key phrases from
"The Practical Approach" section of the book. There's a list of the first
five phrases below, and here's a test of mind control you can try: *Don't
read the list of key phrases until I get to that numbered item—and then don't
read ahead.* [For the presentation, the list was on a flip chart. Here, the
first five items from the flipchart are reproduced in a text box. Remember, don't read the items in the box until you get to the corresponding
points in the presentation.] And while you're doing or not-doing that
test, here are some additional questions to consider:

Q: "Do you think, or do you think that you think?"

That's a brain-teaser that Rose commented on in the *Meditation
Paper.* We identify with our thoughts and desires as if they were our

proud possessions, or sometimes our demons. [All quotes are from *The Psychology of the Observer* unless otherwise noted.]

Q: Do you intentionally start thinking when you awake in the morning? Can you stop thinking? Try it now....

Q: "How does a person realize he or she is not really thinking? We can't stop thinking or start thinking, and we can rarely choose the subject material or the direction of thought."

Q: Do you intentionally select your thoughts? Your feelings? Other objects of consciousness? Do you select the opposing fears and desires that cause your internal conflicts? Do you select your reactions to the above? Do you select their recording and recall?

```
1 - in search of awareness
2 - romance & make-believe
3 - freedom from facing oneself
4 - excessive indulgence of the appetites
5 - destined to do mighty things
```

1. *in search of awareness* [first item on list; you can look at the first item in the box now, but don't read ahead]

Have you ever thought of the search for whatever it is you're looking for in terms of a "search of awareness"? My feeling is that if a person pursues whatever he's searching for deeply enough, it will become a search for the source of his awareness. Rose equated that with an investigation of the self—of the real self or Ultimate Observer. He also referred to it as defining the self.

2. *romance & make-believe*

What do romance or make-believe have to do with controlling the mind? If you watch a child at play, you'll see that we begin indulging in these moods at an early age ... and they stay with us for decades. These particular moods control our minds and encourage a great deal of unrealistic thinking. Rose comments that most people "cast their lives away almost wantonly." Have you observed that?

3. *freedom from facing oneself*

Freedom has the connotation of being good, but it could be counterproductive in this context. If a person is drawn to meditation, I assume it's because of a dissatisfaction they're trying to neutralize.

Such dissatisfaction results from not knowing the self, and to know the self, we have to face the self. But there seems to be great resistance to doing that. And is there a technique for doing it—or are techniques used to procrastinate doing it?

Rose wrote that we need a system that will allow the student to really think, perhaps for the first time. His conviction was that posture doesn't matter. Walking may be best. The important thing is to spend a prescribed period of time alone each day in some manner.

### 4. *excessive indulgence of the appetites*

Indulgence has the connotation of being bad, but it's often the initial catalyst for real self-analysis. You might think it would begin with an adolescent fear of death or the shock of rejection, but generally that doesn't lead to a questioning of what's alive and facing death. It's informative to observe the effect of too-muchness on the body and mind. Rose advised that it also pays to observe others' attitudes toward us and to note the effects of their appetites on their health and peace of mind.

### 5. *destined to do mighty things*

"Almost every young man thinks that he is an outstanding creature, that is destined to do mighty things...."

### 6. *intense appreciation of the self*

He has an "intense appreciation of the self as being unique and of extreme importance to the world"—and typically treats his "family as being secondary or implementive." Sound familiar?

Being successful in one of the life games (e.g., fame, wealth, knowledge; see Robert DeRopp's *Master Game* for a table of object games and metagames) might complicate this delusion, but in any case life is organized to provide what Rose termed "afflictions to the individuality sense" that will challenge this vanity. Life is generous in handing out those incidents, so it's a question of whether we use them in our search for meaning.

### 7. *dynamic search for the permanent center*

What would propel you to a dynamic search for the permanent center of yourself? The bhakti mystic has a feeling for it (Love). The idealist has a desire for it (Truth). The dissatisfied have a longing for it (Reality, Peace, etc.).

What currently prevents it? Hesitation, playing it safe, trying to appease all the desires and fears—that's the mode of procrastinating it. The core reason: the pride of individuality.

8. *lonely in the face of infinity*

Many people feel lonely, and fear of dying alone is a common fear. These are both symptoms of the recognition that we're facing the unknown, infinity. The only comfortable view in the face of infinity comes from the seat of non-transience.

9. *aware that something is aware*

You appear to be a separate individual. Your thoughts are not the same thoughts as your neighbor's. Your inner struggle is not the same as your neighbor's. "Something in [your] consciousness is aware of [your] struggle. Something is aware, and [you are] aware that something is aware."

You are aware that you desire. But do you desire, or are you caused to desire? Do you select things as objects of desire—such as picking the type of person for a mate—or "is all that selection determined by computerizations more intricate than [your] conscious mind is capable of having?"

10. *something within you....*

Something within you "urges and inhibits." Sometimes it causes you to take risks. At other times it results in caution. Something in you causes you to "enter joyously into the game of life"—and at times makes you "long for death."

"And yet all of these things seem to form a pattern, which makes for some sort of destiny. Something within [you], if [you] allow it to, will make decisions for [you], take care of [your] children, and condition [you] for dying when the time comes."

That something is the decision-making program at work. Rose labeled it "the Umpire," which will make perfect sense to you if you see it in operation.

11. *no consideration for your spiritual hopes*

When we observe the decision-making at work, we see that it's apparently programmed to follow a blueprint, a plan of nature, which makes any consideration for our spiritual hopes secondary. It doesn't discourage religion, but it "encourages all religions which encourage nature."

12. *disciplines for spiritual survival*

"… and it draws the blinds of drowsiness over the minds that speculate too long on immortality and the disciplines for guaranteeing spiritual survival."

The quest for permanence is a game that's contra-ego and contra nature's hypnosis. ("We stagger soberly between the blades of the gauntlet with recklessness and conviction, but we pick our way through the tulips with fear and trepidation because the trap of the latter is sweet." Richard Rose, "Notes on Between-ness," *The Direct-Mind Experience.*)

13. *self-aware yet painfully subject to a termination of that consciousness*

Rose points out that we can assume that there must have been some purpose in creating individuals who are "self-aware yet painfully subject to a termination of that consciousness." But the question must remain unanswered for now because:

14. *one job at a time*

"The energy and commitment of the observer can only handle one job at a time"—that job being defining the self, answering the "Who am I?" question.

"Who is living? Who is faced with oblivion?…. Who is asking the question? Who is it that observes the glassy fragments of thought and self, which if sorted and properly arranged, will form some magic crystal ball that shall for all time answer our questions about our future?"

So we puzzle over this unseen self, trying to put the fragments together into some satisfying answer—typically with these results: We get frustrated, angry, discouraged, self-pitying … whatever negative emotions our personality has learned to use to reinforce its tenuous position.

Douglas Harding, in *Look for Yourself:* "How is it that we need all this prodding, all these warnings and earnest invitations and promises of infinite rewards, to persuade us to take a really close look at ourselves? Why don't all intelligent and serious people make it their chief business in life to find out whose life it is?"

15. *is there an adverse force?*

Rose: "Keep to the business of observing. When observation turns into a course of action in regard to adversity, then a religion emerges. And when a religion is formed, dichotomy of the mind follows. In other words, observation is just looking until realization is reached. The only action that should be taken is some form of self-discipline to keep the focus of observation from wandering, or some change in the immediate environment to make thinking easier."

John Wren-Lewis ("Unblocking a Malfunction in Consciousness"): "One thing I learned in my former profession of science was the right kind of lateral thinking can often bring liberation from Catch-22 situations, provided the Catch-22 is faced in its full starkness, without evasions in the form of metaphysical speculations beyond experience."

и

Why control the mind?

There are some obvious practical advantages—doing chores or homework regardless of our mood, for example. But we're here to talk about the search for your awareness. And that's where the topic of meditation comes in. Productive meditation involves using the mind as a stick to stir the fire.

What meditation technique should you use?

o Theory: Self-inquiry is the fast track; devotion the slow path.

o Theory: "Seeing" is the fast, direct path, but we're often diverted at the cloverleaf junction into the way of the devotee, the way of the servant, or the way of the artist. (Douglas Harding, *To Be and not to be* [capitalized as on book cover].)

o Theory: "One should not think of [the Self] with the mind. Such imagination will end in bondage.... Enquiry into the Self in devotional meditation evolves into the state of absorption into the Self and leads to Liberation.... Because the ego in the form of the 'I-thought' is the root of the tree of illusion, even a tree is felled by the cutting of its roots." (Ramana Maharshi, "Self-Enquiry.")

o Theory: Most testimonies have come from people who have found the Truth through the path of feeling. Thus their advice commonly consists of stopping thought. The minority have gotten there through thinking. The fastest route is for the individual to hone whichever faculty—thinking or feeling—is more dominant. (Franklin Merrell-Wolff, *Pathways Through to Space*.)

o Theory: We have two tools to use—common sense and intuition. They need to be employed together, to check each other. (Richard Rose.)

Richard Rose's 4-step technique for controlling the mind ("I do not wish to leave the impression that there an exact number of steps but rather that things should be done with definite preparation and in proper sequence.") in the section on "Controlling the Mind" at the end of *The Psychology of the Observer*:

1. The body has to come under control. Force it to sit ... outwit it by exposing it to tapes or reading, then go for a walk and allow whatever thoughts happen to come.

2. Establish an objective. First realize that thoughts happen on their own, each paving the way for the next. (It may take some "effortless" watching of the mind to reach that realization.) Insert our objective into the seemingly endless chain of thought-caused thoughts. We wish to scrutinize the self.

3. Avoid trying to view the self directly and objectively until the mind is placed under some control. The self is not something that can be imagined or visualized objectively, like a gold nugget. Don't try to visualize an Umpire (the decision-making process), for example. Wait until you know the mind well enough so that the workings we label as the Umpire become overwhelmingly manifest and the mind realizes that no other explanation of those workings is possible than to view it as an Umpire.

4.  The fourth step begins by isolating the mind so that there is nothing else of importance to think about. Surround yourself with pertinent books, tapes, reminders. Make the commitment of step #2—a silent order to the computer that we prefer to think of nothing rather than tolerate rambling, irrelevant thoughts. Thoughts may stop by this technique of turning the head away from irrelevant thoughts. It's important to have a mental vector or philosophic direction established first.

An exercise to try now: Think only of thought…. [Can you do it? For how long?]

"Real concentration at its best is only a very artful way of allowing yourself to think along desired lines," Rose points out.

The four steps provide a framework for getting started, but eventually we come to a point where progress depends on insights gained from our introspection of the mind.

In the *Psychology of the Observer*, Rose has provided examples of how to go about the discovery of the Umpire and then of a Process Observer beyond the Umpire.

He tells us: "The Umpire is discovered by the recognition of polarity in all mundane things, including the mundane mind…. Such a somatic Umpire rules our life until we can build, synthetically, a philosophic Umpire, focused by our desire upon the self for its survival and definition…."

### Suppose Truth Is a Rabbit, by Alfred Pulyan

The truth does not permeate all religions except in such fantastic disguise that its own father wouldn't know it. Suppose truth is a rabbit. This rabbit is in a field—a large field. Round the field are very high walls—creeds and dogma! So—find your damn rabbit!! And remember *the rabbit knows your thoughts* & so as you resolve to go one way to catch it, it knows & evades you!

## *I Am Not Opposed, by Mark Butler*

What does it mean to have "successfully completed the spiritual search"? I am not opposed to the asking of any question. Asking allows one to reason through a problem. However, questions work both ways. They often indicate a lot about the thoughts going on behind the asking. In this case the question provides a wonderful opportunity to really look back at one's self. Not just at the surface to provide an answer but at the very asking itself. Who or what is asking?

"How can a person know if he or someone else—a prospective teacher—has successfully completed the spiritual search?"

Those questions requiring self analysis are most beneficial in progressing on the path to self realization. And so this one is. However, in this case I suggest we look at the other end of the equation. On the surface it makes perfectly good sense to ask this question. Ostensibly the answer would keep one from making some kind of mistake. But let us ask ourselves: What would be the nature of that mistake? Could it be the mistake of continuing to work on our spiritual growth when all is done? Or perhaps the mistake of not setting up shop and teaching others our newly found profound wisdom?

It begins: "How can a person know...." well, by its very definition knowing means just that—Knowing. When one knows something, then there is no question. So what is really being asked here? Could it be whether one's belief is true or not? Let's reword the statement: "I believe that I might have completed my spiritual search, but I am not sure." Often belief and knowing are used interchangeably. However, there is a world of difference between them. Belief is not the same as knowing. In fact, when you really think about it, "belief" amounts to little more than a projection and illusion that we create, perhaps stemming from something that we were told or taught or an assumption based on who knows what. It does not necessarily originate from a genuine personal experience. What is really being asked is "When we believe that we might have 'completed the spiritual search' (i.e., attained 'enlightenment') how can we convince ourselves that we have?" If you have to ask yourself whether you know, you already have your answer.

In whatever form instruction from those teachers generally recognized as having true knowledge is manifest, one consistent injunction is made: to set aside falsehood in any form (beliefs) and the attachments and desires from which they spring. The search is, in fact, the effort to realize and know Truth—the absolute and profound difference between believing (projecting) something and Knowing something. Knowing is an absolute. In short, Knowing has nothing in common with belief.

What does it mean to have "successfully completed the spiritual search"? The question itself presumes a great deal and implies an understanding and knowledge of what the end point is (if there is in fact really an end point). If you have not gotten there, how do you know what there is like? This is one of the very real obstacles on the path to understanding, the subtle implication that we already know what "enlightenment" is. If we believe we already know what the end point is, we will inevitably seek to find it. And, we generally find just what we are looking for, warts and all. This is precisely why spiritual teachers stress "not seeking" as a fundamental aspect of a fruitful spiritual path. Don't chase the illusion!

A dedication to Truth is necessary for a successful spiritual search. A person must be willing to face the truth of their situation. The term brutally honest is not called that for nothing. Honesty, particularly that for ourselves, often feels brutal. So what would be bruised by honesty? Could it be the ego? Again we find if any question remains within the individual as to whether or not they have attained "enlightenment," then they have the answer. They have not reached the journey's end—and so it goes. Honesty with one's self as to belief or knowing is the only valid criteria. The only person that can insure or prevent you from realizing your own true state is *you.*

Which brings us to the next part of the question as regards a prospective teacher—an apt question. Obviously one does not want to waste time and energy fruitlessly listening and following a teacher who does not know what he/she is talking about or, worse yet, is deliberately misleading his/her students. So how do you know? Well you don't. The fact is, there are countless systems, teachers and offerings for every taste you might imagine. If you want to learn how to become wealthy or powerful or how to impress your friends and neighbors by levitating and reading their minds, or how sex can lead to the highest spiritual realization, then there is an instructor for you.

One who is seriously searching must learn to use discernment. There is no doubt the ultimate responsibility for who or what you choose to listen to lies with you and not with the instructor. So how do you safeguard yourself? Well, first off one must learn to be honest with one's self. Ask yourself: What are my true motives? What am I really trying to accomplish? When you are ready to learn any Truth regardless of what it might mean or not mean, then your growing discernment will point you in the most beneficial direction. By the time a person begins to ask themselves, "How can I be sure this or that particular teacher is appropriate to listen to?" they have already begun to use discernment in their search. More significantly, they have already begun to question themselves and everything around them. And this is a most important aspect of the path—the questioning of one's self. If you set your desires and attachments aside and open yourself to honesty, you will see the truth or falsehood that stands behind the words uttered by a prospective teacher.

One aspect alluded to in the proposal statement was the fulfillment of ego death. This is a criterion by which I evaluate both prospective teachers and systems as well as myself. Do they exhibit evidence of egoic motivation? Do they exhibit evidence of desire and attachment in their actions and words? There have been those times when I have experienced profound life altering realizations that I know are essential to understanding the nature of Reality. I too have asked the questions posed in this essay and I have come to realize that when I question whether or not I have accomplished the "goal," I found it was the ego to which I was still responding. It is the ego that calls understanding into question. As long as one responds to an egoic sense of self, the work continues. The ego lies, and if we listen at all to the ego, we are being influenced by and identifying with those lies. In that case we are, in fact, living a lie.

And that brings us to the final aspect of the original question posed this month. After all the realizations and experiences, what seemingly must occur? Ancient as well as more modern teachings specifically describe a death of self. Obviously they are not speaking of a physical death. So what is self? What does a sense of self do? Our egoic sense of self is what separates us from all else. Self is dualism personified. Self is Ego.

We have heard the words so often that they have become cli;chéd: One with all things; nondualism. These words are an attempt to describe a state of being completely different from what is considered "normal" or at least common. So ask your self, what is the one thing that stands in the way?

In our efforts to grow spiritually, we all labor under a lifetime of habit and misinformation. We struggle to recognize these things so that we can then set them aside. Make no mistake, it is hard work. I realize that there is little comfort in these words. But then, the spiritual path is not meant to be comfortable. It certainly disrupts the cozy illusion in which we have participated so willingly, albeit unwittingly. No, it is about Reality and that simply is what it is.

Die while you're alive
and be absolutely dead.
Then do whatever you want: it's all good.
*Bunan (1603 – 1676)*

# About TAT

Richard Rose created the TAT Foundation in 1973 in order to encourage people who were searching for an answer to their deepest life-questions to work together. TAT members, both those who knew Richard Rose personally and newcomers, are continuing those efforts more than thirty years later. We're a community of seekers and finders with four gatherings each year. Individual members sponsor local self-inquiry groups in their areas as well as online groups.

Please visit *www.tatfoundation.org* for more information on our activities. Also, see the August 2005 *TAT Forum* there for a memorial issue dedicated to Richard Rose.

Richard Rose (1917–2005), teacher and friend

# Index and Credits

## *Cartoons*

## *Photographs*